Autism

Autism is the first book that seeks to combine medical, historical, and cultural approaches to an understanding of the condition. Its purpose is to present a rounded portrayal of the ways in which autism is currently represented in the world. It focuses on three broad areas: the facts of scientific research, including new ideas surrounding research into genetics and neuroscience, as well as the details of diagnosis and therapy; the history of the condition as it developed through psychiatric approaches to the rise of parent associations, neurodiversity, and autism advocacy; and the fictional and media narratives through which it is increasingly expressed in the contemporary moment. Accessible and written in clear English, *Autism* is designed for student audiences in English, Disability Studies, Cultural Studies, History, Sociology, and Medicine and Health, as well as medical practitioners and the general reader. Autism is a condition surrounded by misunderstanding and often defined by contestation and argument. The purpose of this book is to bring clarity to the subject of autism across the full range of its manifestations.

Stuart Murray is Professor of Contemporary Literatures and Film and Director of Medical Humanities research in the School of English at the University of Leeds in the UK. He is the author of *Representing Autism: Culture, Narrative, Fascination* (Liverpool UP, 2008) and a number of articles on disability representation.

The Routledge Series Integrating Science and Culture
Editor: Lennard Davis, University of Illinois at Chicago

The Routledge Series Integrating Science and Culture aims to reunite the major discourses of science and the humanities which parted ways about 150 years ago. Each book picks an important topic that can best be understood by a synthesis of the best science and the best social and cultural analysis. In an age when more and more major political and life decisions involve complex understandings of science, medicine, and technology, we need to have a bioculturally sophisticated citizenry who can weigh in on these important issues. To that end these books aim to reach a wide swathe of people, presenting the information in readable, illustrated, succinct editions that are designed for classroom and scholarly use as well as for public consumption.

Forthcoming
Culture by Nicole Anderson
Depression by Bradley Lewis
Sex and Gender by Anne Fausto-Sterling

Autism

Stuart Murray

Routledge
Taylor & Francis Group

NEW YORK AND LONDON

Please visit the companion website at www.routledge.com/textbooks/9780415884990

First published 2012
by Routledge
711 Third Avenue, New York, NY 10017

Simultaneously published in the UK
by Routledge
2 Park Square, Milton Park, Abingdon, Oxon OX14 4RN

Routledge is an imprint of the Taylor & Francis Group, an informa business

© 2012 Taylor & Francis

Library of Congress Cataloging in Publication Data
Murray, Stuart.
  Autism/Stuart Murray.
  p. cm.—(The Routledge series integrating science and culture)
  1. Autism.   I. Title.
  RC553.A88M87 2011
  616.85′882—dc23   2011025819

ISBN13: 978-0-415-88498-3 (hbk)
ISBN13: 978-0-415-88499-0 (pbk)
ISBN13: 978-0-203-80599-2 (ebk)

Typeset in Adobe Caslon and Copperplate by
Florence Production Ltd, Stoodleigh, Devon

Printed and bound in the United States of America
on acid-free paper by Walsworth Publishing Company, Marceline, MO.

SUSTAINABLE
FORESTRY
INITIATIVE

Certified Sourcing
www.sfiprogram.org
SFI-00555
The SFI label applies to the text stock.

For Lucas and Yann—my teachers. Again, but more so . . .

Contents

SERIES FOREWORD

The Routledge Series Integrating Science and Culture aims to restore connections between the sciences and the humanities, connections that were severed over 150 years ago. This mutual exclusion was done in the name of expertise on the part of science and defended in the name of preserving values and morality in the world of humanism. In some sense, each side was seen as the societal enemy of the other. From the humanists' perspective, scientists threatened to make the world a colder, more efficient place lacking in feelings and values. From the scientists' viewpoint, humanists were interfering with progress by injecting bleeding hearts and unreasonable fears into an essentially rational process.

But the reality is that now, in the 21st century it is getting harder and harder for humanists to comment on civic and social matters without knowing something about science, medicine, and technology. Suddenly there is the need to understand stem cells, brain scans, DNA technologies, organ transplants, ecological outcomes, and the like in order to be a knowledgeable citizen, legislator, or scholar. Likewise, scientists routinely include the ethical, social, cultural, and legal in their research protocols and scientific articles. The divide between the "two cultures" described by C.S. Lewis in the 1950s is less and less possible in the 21st century. On the ground, humanists and scientists are again in need of each other.

To that end, the books in this series will focus on the cultural side of science and the scientific side of culture. David Morris and myself have coined the term "biocultural" to indicate this new realm of study and critique. In that spirit, Stuart Murray's book on autism aims to bring together in a truly interdisciplinary sense the best of both knowledges on this pressing social and scientific subject. A proof of the validity of the biocultural claim is that this book, or really any complete book, on autism can only be written using this complex kind of analysis. How much sense would it make to write a book on autism that was purely about the neurological or the biological when the complex phenomenon of autism is best understood in a multi-faceted perspective that includes the social, psychological, political, and scientific? Would it ever be possible to write about autism without including the voices of all parties involved: autists, doctors, parents, and policy makers? How could we understand the network of effects of autism without considering the representations of the condition in the media and in literature and the arts? Murray's book is not an artificial welding of disparate discourses but through its necessary eclecticism offers to give us the best, well-rounded description and explanation of autism to date.

Lennard Davis
Series Editor

PREFACE

My youngest son approaches me with his arms outstretched, asking to be carried. This is unusual; he is 11 years old and this kind of behavior, which was common when he was younger, has by now largely vanished. It is, however, a good opportunity to engage with him physically, something that is not always possible given that frequently he is not keen on being touched; so—telling him how heavy he is (despite the fact that he barely eats anything)—I scoop him up. I stand still: his face is now close to mine, allowing me an excellent opportunity to look closely at him. He draws his arms together between our chests and leans into me, humming and singing and occasionally making surreptitious glances at my face. Then, seeing I'm waiting for further instructions, he leans again, this time to one side, a little nod to the direction he wants me to carry him. It's out to the garden, so off we go, across the patio and up to the steps on to the grass. I stop and, faking the world-weary tone parents always use when they have no clue about their child's wishes, ask him where we're going. Another lean directs me to the trampoline at the back of the garden, although this is not so much an answer to my actual question as a response to the fact that I had stopped walking, a touch of impatience on his part.

Trampolines and autism go together a lot; there is a certain kind of pleasure in the physical sensation, the proprioceptive feedback, which comes with the repetition of the bouncing and the feeling of the body in motion. When he was younger, my son was an endless trampolinist, although his enthusiasm for this has diminished a little as he has grown older. I set off again, telling him that I know full well he is perfectly capable of walking to the trampoline on his own, but in fact loving this chance to be close to him. Stumbling somewhat now, we reach the trampoline and, using his body to make his meaning clear, he asks that I put him on, a request followed by a grab of my hand that signals I'm wanted on there as well. So up I climb. We sit together for about five seconds before it's made clear that I have to get off, get him off, and then carry him back down the garden to the house. We do this whole process twice, a there-and-back trip accompanied each time by various happy burblings and vowel sounds on this part, and by grumbling on mine, before it all stops and he happily lets me go and turns to another activity.

What to make of this event? There are, of course, two versions of it. On my son's part it appears to be a very pleasurable five minutes or so, a succession of moments that leaves him deeply content. Why that might be, what combination of (maybe) physical sensation, memory, and present moment, is for him to know. From my point of view, and despite my faux protestations, it is equally enjoyable, a shared moment of close contact. The question as to whether it is *meaningful* is, I sense, one that seems obvious; the anecdote invites interpretation and reading, it seems to demand to be turned into some kind of 'account.' Despite this being the case, however, the truth is that it probably isn't functioning in this way. Though I might be puzzled by the unusual nature of what happens, a moment of difference within a condition that stresses regular patterns, an interruption in a routine that is normally strictly adhered to, I feel that the temptation to make it somehow symbolic is an error. Too often we assume that autistic behavior comes laden with meaning, that it somehow cannot be as random and casual, as open, as any other behavior. With autism, we want to interpret because *we don't know.* But such interpretation here may well not be necessary in understanding why this small event might be pleasurable, or seeing how it both carries insight and resists analysis. In the way in which it is not symbolic, it is instructive; part of me likes that which stays beyond my reach here, because it is an aspect of my son's character, part of what makes him the complex person he is. And maybe he has his version of the same. The fact that what we both feel can't be completely communicated doesn't mean that it cannot be understood, quite possibly on both sides, and understanding it does not require a complete sense of what it might mean. I sense that an experience such as this is not an uncommon autism episode, and maybe we treat the condition with more respect and integrity if we admit to its inherent openness rather than assume it offers itself up for an interpretation that, in the language of critical analysis, could only be articulated from one perspective anyway, however sensitive that might be.

This book recognizes that understanding and talking about autism is complex. It is written from a point of view that combines scholarly interest and personal experience, but it is unusual in that its perspective is predominantly a non-medical one. Most academic books on autism come from either disciplines associated with Medicine, such as Psychology or Medical History and Sociology, or education-based scholarship. And most general books on the condition are written by psychologists in particular. I have things to say about medicine, psychology, and education, but central to my sense of how we might understand autism is a desire to place the condition in cultural contexts, to see that the various opinions and theories that surround it are part of a wide fabric of narrative, representation, and characterization. This does not mean that the book will abandon the views of medicine to embrace autism as a set of stories, but it does mean that it will see medical research on the condition as one kind of story, and it will stress the benefits of so doing. In what follows I will both question many of the medical and scientific understandings of autism and see others as being central to the way in which we might imagine a future for those who have the condition. A cultural approach to the condition allows for both perspectives, and these are themselves simply part of the larger matrix that we have begun to suspect autism to be.

The desire to understand autism means that, above all things, we want to make sense of it. My anecdote above suggests, however, that this may not necessarily be the right approach. Maybe it is better to say that those who are not autistic want to engage with autism, and although this may well be difficult, it is also a situation that is potentially hugely productive. In addition, it is not one in which we need to rush into interpretations of what the condition is. Autism is frequently talked about, but it is rarely listened to. In wanting to integrate scientific and cultural attitudes towards the facts that surround the condition, we need to articulate more theories, and bring to bear more methods of enquiry, than we do at the current moment. One of these is an approach that seeks to critique the dominant and orthodox sense of what we think we know; another is the belief that there is much from autism that we can learn. My goal in writing this book is that it will be able to help with both.

As anyone connected to autism knows, and as every member of an English department will assert, language matters. The language surrounding autism, and disability more generally, is itself often a minefield full of argument and opinion. Many claim that the term 'autistic person' is demeaning, because it suggests that the individual concerned is somehow defined by their autism, and that this is prejudiced and problematic. For the majority who work in social or healthcare, and in education, the phrase 'person with autism' is preferred, since it indicates a removal of any such stigma. At the same time, however, the 'autistic person' label is one used by many people with the condition precisely because they do consider their autism part of their being, and there is also the potential problem with 'person with autism' that it suggests—too easily—that the autism might be removed from the person, as if to have autism is to have a cold or some disease. I can see both sides of the argument, and so this book uses both terms, not in any strict way but rather as they came to me in the writing. Some readers may well feel that these concerns over vocabulary are pedantic and fussy, and that it really doesn't matter which phrase is used. But, as we will see, the ways in which autism is talked about are vital if we are to understand how we think of the condition at this moment in time; and if it seems that this is part of an over-sensitive argument, this book will show that arguments about autism are integral to our contemporary discussions, and that sensitivity is equally important. In the end, my use of language in the book, as with all other aspects of its content, is directed towards a greater understanding of, and interaction with, autism. That desire is the baseline for everything that follows.

ACKNOWLEDGMENTS

I am very grateful to Lennard Davis for the initial conversation which led to the development of this book, and for all his support through the writing and publication process. Thanks to the staff at Routledge in New York as well and to the readers of the manuscript, Ralph Savarese of Grinnell College and Joseph Straus of CUNY Graduate Center. I would like to thank all the various individuals and associations that provided me with material and details which went into the book, especially the National Autistic Society, the Wellcome Trust, Stephen Wiltshire and family, Michael Baron, Indrani Basu, Bridget Bennett, and Ralph Smith. In September 2010, as I was working on the book, I was invited by Michael Orsini and Joyce Davidson to speak at a Critical Autism Workshop in Ottawa, and I would want to thank all the participants there, but especially Michael and Joyce, for the stimulating environment that event produced.

I owe longstanding debts to Clare Barker, Kirsty Bennett, and John McLeod for their friendship and support, which goes beyond the writing of books. Kevin, Marion, and Tim McLoughlin make the most wonderfully supportive of families and I would especially want to thank them for helping me to find time to work in Cornwall in the summer of 2010. This book is, of course, for the boys, but it is for Megan as well, without whom there would be no way in which I could write at all.

Stuart Murray
Leeds, December 2010

PART I
THE FACTS

1 What We Know . . . or Don't

We know more about autism now than at any point in history. We know that it is a neurodevelopmental condition, which is almost certainly biogenetic in origin, and that it affects the ways in which information is processed in the brain. We know that, whatever the debates surrounding ideas of treatment and cure, it is a lifelong condition, and that it affects far more people than was believed even 10 years ago. We know that autism is a spectrum condition, and as such takes many forms, from the non-verbal to the highly talkative for example, or from those who revel in sensory stimuli to those who find such encounters painful and distressing. We know that there seems to be more autism about, that the condition is diagnosed, highlighted, discussed, and represented as never before, even though we also know that there have always been people with autism but that we chose not to label them as such until the recent past. We know that most people with autism are considered disabled but that some choose to see themselves rather in terms of difference, and reject the idea that they 'suffer from' their condition. We know all these things and more, and yet at the same time, if we're honest, the foundational observation we might make, the 'central fact' about autism with which we should probably start, is that we don't know very much about it at all.

We don't know what causes autism. For all that neurology continues to help us understand how the brain is the site of the condition, we don't know fully which brain areas are responsible for the ways in which those with autism process their experiences of the world. Equally, despite advances in research on genetics, we have no real idea which genes are those connected to autism. We have established methods that enable us to diagnose the condition, processes of specialist observation that work through reference to established guidelines, but we don't know if such techniques are the best way for us to identify the manner in which autism manifests itself in any one individual; we simply believe them to be the most useful at this present moment in time. We don't know whether environmental factors play a part in autism or, if they do, how we might establish the extent to which this is the case. And, putting two of our 'don't knows' together, we don't know if, or how, possible genetic and environmental factors interact, though some suspect that they might. Lastly, given that much of what we do know about autism comes from recent research, we don't know much about autism and the future. We know very little about the condition and ageing, for example, and (to discuss the issue in different terms) we don't know what the future will need in terms of educational or social healthcare policies for those with autism.

In this first section, I want to extend this question of 'what we know' and outline and explore the 'facts' of autism. I want especially to discuss the condition as it is understood by medical knowledge, and the ways in which the terms of such understanding have created a sense of what the condition is and how it works in the world. When the word 'autism' is mentioned, I suspect that there is an immediate and seemingly natural assumption that the point of departure for further thinking about what it is, the first frame in which to consider it, is that of the medical. Autism is, after all, often referred to as a 'condition,' frequently a 'disorder,' and sometimes a 'disease,' and we believe these terms to be foremostly medical: medical research into genes and the workings of the brain helps us to further the understanding of autism's genetic patterning and its neurological make-up, and medical practice in terms of psychology and healthcare aid in the diagnosis and ongoing support of those who are autistic. Medicine is, it appears, our best guide for understanding autism at any given moment in time; medical research is vital in determining what autism is and how it functions. As we will see later in this book, it has played a significant role in alleviating some of the controversies and fanciful notions that surround the condition.

And yet we need to juxtapose our faith in the competency of medical knowledge and its methods with the limitations of such knowledge mentioned above. We need to understand that, when faced with the complexities of what constitutes autism, medical thinking is *necessarily* speculative, that it creates narratives of enquiry that allow for research or practice to function. Such processes, in turn, mean that the picture of autism that emerges from the various lenses of medical activity, for all that it is essential, is a partial one that contains its own emphases and biases. As vaccine expert Paul Offit says in *Autism's False Prophets*, his book on many of the debates surrounding the condition in the last decade: "People think of science as a body of knowledge or scientific societies or scientists. But it's really just a way of thinking about a problem" (Offit 2008, 206). If we are to gain a true sense of what autism means to us in the here and now, we have to accept the provisional nature of much medical investigation, its 'way of thinking,' even as we look to it for the clues that will enable us to know more about what makes up the condition. We have to ask hard questions about what the 'facts' of autism really are.

2 The Body, the Brain, and the Person

Biology, Neurology, and Self

Much current medical research into the origins of autism centers on the idea of brain difference and what is sometimes termed 'atypical brain structure.' In recent years, advances in the ability to study living brains (as opposed to those accessed only through autopsy) through magnetic resonance imagery (MRI), and especially the opportunities provided by functional magnetic resonance imagery (fMRI) to follow the workings of the brain as it is engaged in a task or problem solving, have allowed for a number of suggestions as to the possible neurological details of autism. Studies show that the brains of those with autism sometimes work in ways that are noticeably different to those who are not autistic, and especially that specific brain regions work differently across a range of individuals.

Science has shown that what is sometimes referred to as 'the social brain,' which includes the medial prefrontal cortex and the amygdala, is frequently 'underactive' in the brains of those with autism. Equally, studies have produced evidence that autistic brains are literally differently

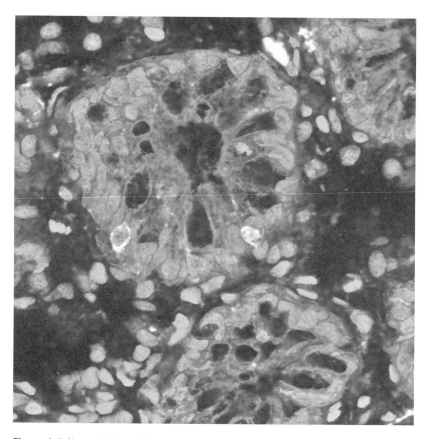

Figure 1.1 Neuroendocrine cells, the pathways of which are thought to function differently in the autistic brain

© S. Schuller/Wellcome Images

shaped to those of individuals without autism. In the two to three years following birth, the brains of those who have autism grow far more rapidly than brains in those children who are not autistic, and on average autistic brains are bigger and heavier than those that show no signs of the condition.

In addition and possibly related to these questions of activity and size, there is increased cell density in certain parts of the brains, the hippocampus and amygdala included, of those with autism, along with other structural differences in the cerebellum, and a noticeable increase in connections between brain neurons (called dendrites). Some young children with autism have what is termed an 'overgrowth' of white and gray matter in the brain's frontal lobes, although this rate of growth, especially of white matter, then seems to fall away as they grow up. Given that gray and white matter is the material which makes up nerve cells and connections, this research (and the other studies on brain structure and function) has led to the hypothesis that the physical make-up of the brain can show us that it is the processes of *connectivity* that are different in autism, and that this can be traced to specific brain areas. In August 2010 the national press in the UK widely reported the details from an article in the *Journal of Neuroscience*, in which scientists at King's College in London outlined their development of a brain scanning technique that could, by 2012, provide a screening process that will aid in the processes of diagnosis (Ecker et al. 2010; Rose 2010). The scan works by providing images of thousands of brain regions, as opposed to individual areas, increasing the chances of developing a holistic sense of the brains of those with autism.

All of this neurobiological research, and accompanying work done on genetics, is done in the name of etiology, the study of the *cause* of diseases. It is a slow and complex business of investigation, and for all the advances that have been made it is wise to remember that the exact nature of how they might contribute to the make-up of autism is still an issue for conjecture. Knowing that brain structure or activity is different in those with autism does not locate this knowledge as a foundational cause of the condition; it does not necessarily clarify *at what point* in the complexities of autism such evidence is most usefully positioned. In thinking about the origins of autism, it is better to conceive of a maze to be negotiated than of a situation where X might mark the spot in terms of causation, and as such the evidence supplied by neurobiological and gene-based research still needs to be inserted in the right context, to be lined up in the right manner with other factors. Does, for example, knowing that the siblings of children with autism have up to a 7 percent probability of also being on the autistic spectrum (a huge increase over that expected in the general population), or being able to identify certain gene combinations as potential 'risk clusters,' give us information that should be considered before or after, as more or less important, than research on the brain? For all the medical research facts we have about autism, knowing in which order they might come remains a problem that has, as yet, no solution.

There is another consequence of the increased medical and scientific research into autism, one that would, in all probability, not really interest those engaged in such work for whom it might not appear relevant. It is to do with the *idea* of the condition that is produced as a result of such concentration, and especially that idea in relation to a sense of personhood or self. Increasingly, we have grown used to the kinds of images produced by MRI processes; we have seen the 'cross sections' of the brain with various parts highlighted in different colors—red or green—and, even though these are not actual photographs but are rather images produced through the conversion of statistical information, we understand them in terms of the way that they signify activity or work, as actual snapshots of the brain in performance. The notion that autism might somehow be found *there*, in those colored patches, is very different from previous conceptions of the condition, where it was more common to assume that the individual person *hosted* his/her autism in some way. I will outline the history of the development of medical thought about autism fully in Part II, but it is worth noting here that the increasing turn to neurological and genetic explanations of the condition replaces a considerable body of work that assumed that autism was psychogenic in origin, that its causes were to be found in the mind. In thinking about autism, this movement from psychology to neurology leaves the question of how the actual *person* with autism might best be considered as a difficult one. Highlighting the issue of connectivity in brain cells is an obvious part of necessary neurobiological research, but its emphasis on 'connections' works to reinforce some common ideas about autism that are in fact cultural in origin; that it can be conceived of in terms of 'processes' or 'wiring,' for example, or that the autistic brain is like a computer's hard drive. The flashing colors of MRI scans further such links of course, appearing as a seemingly literal manifestation of the approach that sees autism as some form of technology. In fact, we should view such depictions of the condition as social and cultural terms formed by the trickle down of scientific thought into a broad-based media, and then into the realm of public debate. This is a subtle observation, and might not be considered as a 'fact' in the same way that research into mirror neurons evidently appears to be, but it is nonetheless a product of the latest medical work on autism that transforms how we think of the condition in ways that may not have been anticipated.

It is in thinking through the consequences of this for the person with autism that we might most profitably understand the way in which the condition has become characterized by science and medicine. After all, autism is only of interest because of the fact that it affects people, and if we cannot extend what we know about it to make a real difference to individual lives then there is not much point to any research on the condition. Thinking of the autistic brain as some kind of computer provides a shorthand to understanding certain elements of neurological connectivity, but it also arguably serves to perpetuate a number of the common stereotypes of people with autism, that they are automatons, for example, somehow robotic, or even that they are 'alien' and in some way non-human, issues I will expand upon in Part III of this book. To make the issue clearer by coming at it from another direction, we might also note that the dominance of a clinical scientific approach to autism makes it easy for other types of questions about the condition to drop off the agenda—how do individuals with autism express their spirituality, for example? Or, what kind of parent does an autistic adult make? That people with autism can be religious is obviously a fact, but in a medicalized arena in which the condition is regularly discussed in terms of being an 'abnormality,' or dominated by the idea that it constitutes a 'deficit,' it can lose the status it should rightly occupy.

The idea of an 'autistic person' then, or an 'autistic self,' is one that can be lost within the micro-details of the latest scientific research. The 'facts' of such research tend to abstract the condition from its connection

Figure 1.2 Further research into the structure of DNA is expected to provide more detail as to the nature of autism

to people, to make it into an object of enquiry. Of course this is the way that medicine necessarily works, but I think that, because we do know that autism is intimately connected to the very foundations of some people's personality, we can immediately see that there is a difference between a person with autism and, say, a person with cancer (another medical condition that is abstracted and objectified in popular discussion). In part, the very idea of an autistic person is a philosophical one, and recent work in Philosophy has started to explore what Deborah R. Barnbaum has termed "autistic integrity" (Barnbaum 2008, 204) as a valid and ethical notion of autistic difference, discussing the concept of an autistic sense of self and a lived life ordered by that self. But the person with autism is also obviously a social individual—family and community member, employee and workmate—and a potential danger of the abstraction of the condition produced by current formations of medical research is that links to the normality of autism, the fact of it understood in terms of daily living and of the everyday, can too easily be lost. It is worth remembering that, for nearly all of us, autism is far more likely to be encountered in a social situation—family, school, college, or work—than in the rarefied atmosphere of a research laboratory.

Medical conceptions of autism also necessarily project the condition into an idea of the future in which more research, more knowledge and facts, will transform it for the better. This is in truth not so much a case of how medical research, which is as haphazard as any other, actually works but rather how it is *seen* to work by a broad public. Mapping the risk genes that might be associated with autism, for example, for all that such work is very much in its first halting phases, appears crucial and meaningful. This is because there is a public consensus that increased knowledge about such genes will improve our wider understanding of the condition, and consequently of the lives of those associated with it. At the same time, however, and as we will see in Part III it is equally likely that the outcome of such genetic research will be the controversial possibility of prenatal screening. In addition, if we pause on the logic of meaningful 'progressive' research for a second, we can see that it is rather curious; it might be obvious that an improvement in the quality of people's lives will come more quickly not with high-level medical science, but rather with improved education or with increased public spending on disability programs for example, given that these are arguably more concrete, and almost certainly faster, ways to raise consciousness and produce discernable results. In addition, the idea of improvement in the future automatically characterizes autism in the present as first and foremostly a 'problem' and something that *requires* change. That this is, in some cases, true is beyond question, but it is the nature of medical research's gesture towards the future here, its claim to make lives better, that runs the risk of stopping us from asking exactly what autistic lives are like in the here and now.

Although much of the above offers a critique of the methods of much medical research in assessing autism, the debate about such methods does of course go on within the scientific research community as well. Scientists such as Laurent Mottron and Michelle Dawson (who is herself autistic) have produced work that seeks to revise what medical research understands by autistic intelligence and perception in particular (Dawson et al. 2005; Mottron et al. 2006). As both have noted, often the very structure of research questions about autism *presumes* that it is a condition of deficit (in, for example, the use of scales of intelligence in measuring autistic capabilities). Equally, Dawson and Mottron, along with colleague Jemel Bouthiena, have challenged the trend in recent autism research that has focused on the ability of those with the condition to process social information through the recognition of facial expressions. This 'face processing' has been seen as a marked advance in recent science on autism, but Bouthiena, Mottron, and Dawson, in a review of the empirical evidence on the topic, have demonstrated that the abilities of autistics to read facial expressions has been seriously underestimated because of the techniques used (Bouthiena et al. 2006). Here, the 'facts' of mainstream contemporary scientific knowledge are not only challenged from a culturalist perspective that sees them as part of the telling of a certain kind of story, they are also revised from within by researchers reviewing evidence and data.

The facts of medical research into autism are, then, more complex than they might seem at first, but it is actually not the research arena in which medicine's interaction with autism is most of interest. That space properly belongs to the business of diagnosing the condition, to the processes involved in the decision making surrounding who does, and who does not, have autism. And it is the question of the *decision* that is so vital here. The brain scan techniques being developed at King's College London may well herald a breakthrough, but as yet—unlike other conditions affecting cognitive processes, such as Down Syndrome or Huntington's disease—there are no biological markers for autism, neurological or otherwise. Consequently there is no straightforward way in which its presence can be read. Because of this, at the moment diagnosis is an evaluative process that nearly always requires the work of more than one specialist. This process is about discussion, opinion, consideration, and the construction of a narrative that surrounds the individual, and as such, its status as a 'fact' is obviously less than clear. Nevertheless, most people with autism are understood to be autistic because they have been diagnosed as such, so its central nature in any discussion of the condition needs to be explored if we are to know quite what we mean when we choose to apply the term.

3 The Detail of Diagnosis

The diagnosis of autism is a complex business. In his small book on the condition, largely aimed at parents of children who are either thinking of going through, or have just undergone, the process of diagnosis, developmental psychopathologist Simon Baron-Cohen provides a thorough survey of what is involved in the evaluation. He writes that it "is often carried out by a multidisciplinary team, typically taking 2 or 3 hours based on interview and observation" (Baron-Cohen 2008, 37). The interview, he notes, will probably be conducted by "a child psychiatrist, clinical or educational psychologist, pediatrician or other health professional" (Baron-Cohen 2008, 38), and he gives some examples of the kinds of questions parents might be asked about their children in order to produce evidence that will aid the diagnostic evaluation. These include queries such as: "Have they found it difficult to make and keep friends?"; "Do they show a lack of normal social awareness?"; "Does the person have trouble understanding non-literal language (such as humor, sarcasm, irony, and metaphor)?"; "Does the person frequently say (as well as do) the wrong thing in a social situation (committing *faux pas*)?"; and "Do they resist change?" (Baron-Cohen 2008, 38–39). It should also be noted that, frequently, a single interview is insufficient to gather all the information needed for diagnosis, and that, following the interview and evaluation processes, the specialist team is often required to meet to produce the agreed decision.

Baron-Cohen's full detailed list of the questions and topics that might be covered in any diagnostic interview is comprehensive, covering nearly two-and-a-half pages of his book. Any parent coming to it, in advance of such an appointment, would feel empowered through access to this kind of knowledge. And yet, for all that this might seem to communicate a process full of precision, Baron-Cohen himself admits that this is really not necessarily the case. He observes:

> One day, the hope is that accurate diagnosis will not depend on the vagaries of a clinical interview or of direct observations of behavior, which invariably includes some subjective elements. Instead, it will be based on a biological marker or set of markers (e.g. a combination of specific gene variants, or a combination of specific protein levels), measured in the blood and in other bodily tissue or cells. But, for now, such a set of biological markers for autism or Asperger syndrome is not yet available, so we need to continue to rely on behavioral and interview-based methods.
>
> (Baron-Cohen 2008, 41)

'Vagaries' is the key word here, even more so than 'subjective.' The shifting terrain of what passes at any given time for knowledge about autism (once again, that which we 'don't know') conditions the implementation of the diagnostic method; it is a classic example of a medical 'best practice' moment, one in which the expertise of the here and now is enacted even as that specialist knowledge necessarily admits to its limits. In her book on diagnosis, Lisa Sanders entitles her first chapter 'The Facts, and What Lies Beyond,' picking up on exactly this limitation inherent in the search for diagnostic precision. To ascertain "more than just the facts" (L. Sanders 2010, 6) is, Sanders claims, vital for proper diagnosis. She asserts that the central element necessary in such a process is the 'patient story,' noting that "the great majority of medical diagnoses—anywhere from 70 to 90 percent—are made on the basis of the patient's story alone." However, as she then observes:

> Although this is well established, far too often neither the doctor nor the patient seems to appreciate the importance of what the patient has to say in the making of a diagnosis. And yet this is crucial information. None of our high-tech tests has such a high batting average. Neither does the physical exam. Nor is there any other way to obtain this information. Talking to the patient more often than not provides the essential clues to making a diagnosis.
>
> (L. Sanders 2010, 7)

With autism, of course, the whole notion of the 'patient story' is complicated. Often clinicians are asked to assess non-verbal children in the context of conversations with their families, although this is less the case with the diagnosis of Asperger's Syndrome where the kinds of dialogue of which Sanders speaks are more possible. It remains true, however, that in the frequent *absence* of the 'patient story' for the individual with autism the narrative is then supplied by the diagnostic method itself, which inevitably fills in the gaps with which it finds itself faced. In fact, if we return to Baron-Cohen's formation (as evidenced by some of the quotations above), what arguably emerges as being most interesting about the business of diagnosis is the combination of medical authority with the narrative *characterization* of the condition, especially in as much as it works towards the creation of what we might term 'autism as a problem.' Looking back on Baron-Cohen's list, it becomes readily apparent that it is full of descriptions of 'difficulties,' 'limitations,' and assumptions about behavior being 'wrong' or deviating from that which is considered 'normal.' And here, the point we need to remember is that this is an account of the expert baseline judgments involved in deciding if any individual does, or does not, have autism. It is crucial to understand that the idea of autism as a 'problem' or 'deficit' is in fact built in, during diagnostic evaluation, to the definition of what the condition is perceived to be.

*is the world's fastest growing
developmental disability.*

People on the autism spectrum may:

✓ not understand what you say
✓ appear deaf
✓ be unable to speak or speak with difficulty
✓ engage in repetitive behaviors
✓ act upset for no apparent reason
✓ appear insensitive to pain
✓ appear anxious or nervous
✓ dart away from you unexpectedly
✓ engage in self-stimulating behaviors
  (i.e., hand flapping or rocking)

*For law enforcement or medical emergency
personnel: This individual may not understand
the law, know right from wrong, or know the
consequences of his or her actions.*

Safe & Sound
AUTISM SOCIETY

Figure 1.3a Autism Society card giving details of behavior
© Autism Society

Autism Society

Helpful hints for interacting with someone who has autism:

✓ Speak slowly and use simple language
✓ Use concrete terms
✓ Repeat simple questions
✓ Allow time for responses
✓ Give lots of praise
✓ Do not attempt to physically block self-stimulating behavior
✓ Remember that each individual with autism is unique and may act differently than others

AUTISM SOCIETY

1-800-3-AUTISM
www.autism-society.org

Figure 1.3b Autism Society card giving details of behavior
© Autism Society

To observe this is not simply to participate in a process of pedantry. The idea that autism—an abstraction seemingly impossible to fully locate or define—becomes *produced* through the processes of diagnosis has obvious consequences for the ways in which the condition is subsequently read in the world. If the language of evaluation begins with built-in assumptions about the 'problems' of autistic behavior, or assumes that discussion of a 'deficit' is natural, then it will always be difficult to view any individual with autism outside of these central frames of reference. If it becomes foundational to conceive of autism as an abnormality then not only does it appear rational that the condition is one that requires 'correction,' it also makes the idea of 'everyday autism,' the daily business of a life lived being autistic, one that is difficult for any individual to sustain or justify.

The list of questions and topics given by Baron-Cohen outlines the types of subjects that may well come up for consideration during diagnosis, but the evaluation team will not have simply assembled its own version of such criteria to assist its work. The yardsticks that guide the diagnosis of autism appear in what we might recognize as the twin 'bibles' of such processes, the American Psychiatric Association's *Diagnosis and Statistical Manual of Mental Disorders* (*DSM*), used especially in North America, and the World Health Organization's *International Classification of Diseases* (*ICD*), with a usage in much of the rest of the world. Each of these texts is published as an authoritative guide, and is then subject to revision before a completely new version is produced; so, for example, the current 'working' model of *DSM* is *DSM-IV*, published in 1994, and then updated as *DSM-IV-TR* in 2000. The new full edition of the manual, *DSM-V*, is scheduled to appear in 2012. With the *ICD*, the current version is *ICD-10*, the tenth revision of a manual that has its origins in the nineteenth century. It has annual updates approved by regular meetings of WHO officials.

In each classificatory system, autism is defined and described in a manner designed to aid any clinician make a diagnosis. As a consequence, these definitions can quite rightly be considered the central diagnostic 'facts' of autism, and are worth reproducing here for our consideration. In *DSM-IV*, the description of autism is separate from that for Asperger's Syndrome and comes under the heading of 'Autistic

Disorders.' The detailed list below is of behaviors, a number of which have to be present for diagnosis to be made:

A. A total of six (or more) items from (1), (2), and (3), with at least two from (1), and one each from (2) and (3):

(1) qualitative impairment in social interaction, as manifested by at least two of the following:

(a) marked impairment in the use of multiple nonverbal behaviors such as eye-to-eye gaze, facial expression, body postures, and gestures to regulate social interaction

(b) failure to develop peer relationships appropriate to developmental level

(c) a lack of spontaneous seeking to share enjoyment, interests, or achievements with other people (e.g., by a lack of showing, bringing, or pointing out objects of interest)

(d) lack of social or emotional reciprocity

(2) qualitative impairments in communication as manifested by at least one of the following:

(a) delay in, or total lack of, the development of spoken language (not accompanied by an attempt to compensate through alternative modes of communication such as gesture or mime)

(b) in individuals with adequate speech, marked impairment in the ability to initiate or sustain a conversation with others

(c) stereotyped and repetitive use of language or idiosyncratic language

(d) lack of varied, spontaneous make-believe play or social imitative play appropriate to developmental level

(3) restricted repetitive and stereotyped patterns of behavior, interests, and activities, as manifested by at least one of the following:

(a) encompassing preoccupation with one or more stereotyped and restricted patterns of interest that is abnormal either in intensity or focus

(b) apparently inflexible adherence to specific, nonfunctional routines or rituals

(c) stereotyped and repetitive motor mannerisms (e.g., hand or finger flapping or twisting, or complex whole-body movements)

(d) persistent preoccupation with parts of objects

B.   Delays or abnormal functioning in at least one of the following areas, with
     onset prior to age 3 years: (1) social interaction, (2) language as used in
     social communication, or (3) symbolic or imaginative play.

C.   The disturbance is not better accounted for by Rett's Disorder or Childhood
     Disintegrative Disorder (*DSM-IV-TR* 2000, 75).
                        (Reprinted with permission from the Diagnostic and Statistical
                             Manual of Mental Disorders, Fourth Edition, Text Revision
                                  (© 2000). American Psychiatric Association)

In the WHO formation, autism is included in the category
'Disorders of psychological development,' which itself is a subset of
'Mental and behavioral disorders' and includes what is termed 'pervasive
developmental disorders' alongside two separate forms of autism,
'childhood autism' and 'atypical autism,' as well as Asperger's Syndrome.
As well as a variant of the kind of diagnostic checklist provided in the
DSM, *ICD-10* also contains prose descriptions of each condition, as
follows:

Childhood Autism

A type of pervasive developmental disorder that is defined by: (a) the presence
of abnormal or impaired development that is manifest before the age of three
years, and (b) the characteristic type of abnormal functioning in all the
three areas of psychopathology: reciprocal social interaction, communication,
and restricted, stereotyped, repetitive behavior. In addition to these specific
diagnostic features, a range of other nonspecific problems are common,
such as phobias, sleeping and eating disturbances, temper tantrums, and
(self-directed) aggression.

Atypical Autism

A type of pervasive developmental disorder that differs from childhood autism
either in age of onset or in failing to fulfil all three sets of diagnostic criteria.
This subcategory should be used when there is abnormal and impaired
development that is present only after age three years, and a lack of sufficient
demonstrable abnormalities in one or two of the three areas of psychopathology
required for the diagnosis of autism (namely, reciprocal social interactions,
communication, and restricted, stereotyped, repetitive behavior) in spite of
characteristic abnormalities in the other area(s). Atypical autism arises most
often in profoundly retarded individuals and in individuals with a severe specific
developmental disorder of receptive language.

Asperger's Syndrome

A disorder of uncertain nosological validity, characterized by the same type of qualitative abnormalities of reciprocal social interaction that typify autism, together with a restricted, stereotyped, repetitive repertoire of interests and activities. It differs from autism primarily in the fact that there is no general delay or retardation in language or in cognitive development. This disorder is often associated with marked clumsiness. There is a strong tendency for the abnormalities to persist into adolescence and adult life. Psychotic episodes occasionally occur in early adult life.

(*ICD-10* 2009, 360–62)

The different kinds of description work in different ways. The *DSM-IV* example here provides a literal checklist that can be followed by any health professional making a diagnosis. The *ICD-10* definitions here display how such manuals also give all-round surveys of differing forms of autism. In its own way, however, each type of prose contains the latest knowledge about autism, offering an update on the history of the condition as it has moved through different levels of understanding (we can look back and see, for example, that it was in only in *DSM-III*, published in 1980, that autism was differentiated from childhood psychosis and considered as a condition in its own right). These accounts are informative, and yet precisely because autism remains symptomatic and is something that has to be pieced together through a reading of any individual within the above observational phrases, we can see that that the diagnostic classifications actually work to paint a certain kind of picture of *how* an individual with autism is characterized. The ways in which the evaluated individual emerges through the diagnostic prose is clearly an activity driven by value judgments.

First, it is evident that the ways in which autism is considered a differentiation from the medical norm are all associated with the negative. Just to take the *DSM-IV* nomenclature, the language of 'impairment' is centered around examples of listed 'failure,' 'lack,' 'delay,' 'stereotyped,' 'repetitive,' 'restricted,' 'inflexible,' 'nonfunctional,' 'disturbance,' and 'abnormal' behaviors. This is the full blown 'autism as deficit' model in operation. Second, because of the working nature of both the *DSM* and the *ICD* definitions, their status as guides for the clinicians using them, they have to be seen as documents that create

diagnosis as a *process* in which the things that are looked for, the signs
of the autism as it were, are located and understood within this deficit
model. The 'abnormality' of which both manuals speak is here grounded
as a difference that can only be read within the logic of the condition
as a problem. And, given that it is always the case that you tend to see
what you are asked to look for, the reality is that autism is created as
a phenomenon that is presented and understood within such terms.

If such a claim seems a touch excessive, we can return to Baron-
Cohen's study to see how the logic of reading diagnosis in this fashion
plays itself out. As a researcher, Baron-Cohen has himself been
instrumental in producing models and techniques that aid diagnosis
through what he terms a process of 'measuring' autism. The Autism
Spectrum Quotient (AQ) that he and his research team at the
University of Cambridge have produced is a method for quantifying
autistic traits in both children and adults. Through the use of a
questionnaire, it calculates a 'score' for any individual that might suggest
a referral for a diagnosis is warranted. But, in expanding on how an
AQ score might be used, Baron-Cohen makes a startling statement
that shows the ways in which the deficit model of autism becomes
easily conflated with ideas about how the condition then manifests
itself within any one individual. He writes:

> A high AQ score alone is not a reason to be referred for a
> diagnosis. In addition, there has to be evidence that the person
> is "suffering" in some way (e.g. they are being bullied, or are
> becoming depressed, or have high levels of anxiety, or are not
> fulfilling their academic or occupational potential).
>
> (Baron-Cohen 2008, 29)

It is a point Baron-Cohen goes on to repeat—"a diagnosis is only
given if a person is *suffering* to some degree" (Baron-Cohen 2008, 32,
emphasis in original)—where 'suffering' is the vital variant in the
otherwise quasi-empirical process of measurement and assessment that
he is advocating in the use of an AQ score as a screening instrument
to aid diagnosis.

It is worth pausing to consider exactly what this means. The idea that
those with autism 'suffer' from the condition is not new; the word is

often used as an active verb to describe any number of disabilities. But Baron-Cohen's observation here is that suffering is *integral* to the manifestation of the condition and subsequent diagnostic process, that it is one of the ways by which autism is properly known. Such a presumption has to be seen as an extraordinary projection from the 'fact' of neurobiological difference that medical research on autism supposes, and it is worth noting that there is no mentioning of suffering in either the *DSM-IV* or the *ICD* definitions. At the same time, we might think that it is explicable that the problem/deficit model at work in both manuals can lead to the kind of slippage that assumes that 'absence' must somehow equal 'suffering,' given that the language itself appears to invite the connection. If there are so many repetitions of 'difficulties' then the idea that suffering must follow seems logical. This explains how Baron-Cohen, a figure who is not unsympathetic to the idea of autism as cognitive difference, can employ language that arrives at this position. It may well be that the meaning intended in his comments is one about process; that it is unusual to give a diagnosis unless the individual presenting to the clinician is identified with a problem, and that those with clear markers of autism who appear untroubled will not be diagnosed because there is no *need* to do so. But, even if this is the case, the obviousness of the structural place suffering or difficulty occupies in this formation of autism cannot be avoided, and is problematic.

To make these points is not to deny that, at times, the experience of autism does include suffering; this much is clear to anyone with any understanding of the condition. Those who are autistic often experience problems, physical and social, in responding to the world around them, and the families of those with autism frequently experience worry and distress. But two reflections immediately spring to mind with respect to this: first, to observe this about autism is not necessarily to make any kind of distinctive claim; after all, other experiences—from poverty to bereavement (and all manner of other life events)—can also clearly cause 'suffering,' and we see no reason to produce individualized diagnostic criteria for these; and second, the fact that for Baron-Cohen the *presupposition* of suffering is a structural part of the evaluative process of autism produces a working version of the condition that has an assumed negativity and a normalized value-judgment built into its medical/diagnostic baseline.

And Baron-Cohen is not alone in making such a claim. In her 'very short introduction' to autism, a book designed to have a wide circulation, cognitive neuroscientist Uta Frith, one of the acknowledged experts on the psychology of the condition, invokes a similar idea in her dismissal of those who might choose to see autism in terms of cognitive difference:

> Some campaigners . . . say that for the whole of the autism spectrum it is wrong to talk of brain abnormalities, wrong to focus on deficits in the mind, and wrong to highlight impairments in behavior. Instead, there should only be talk of differences in brain and mental make-up, some of which represent the autistic mind. This is a strange proposition. To someone who is familiar with classic cases and other severe cases of autism, and knows of the suffering that is associated with autism, it seems perverse.
>
> (Frith 2008, 37–38)

Figure 1.4 Uta Frith
© Anne-Katrin Purkiss/Wellcome Images

"You may disagree," Frith continues, "but then this book is not for you" (Frith 2008, 38), an intriguing comment in a book (like this one you are reading) designed for a wide readership. It may be that Frith is thinking of the experiences of parents here, given that autism is mainly diagnosed in childhood, but even if this is the case the reiteration of the centrality of suffering, and the notion that to oppose it is 'perverse,' are striking examples of the full force of the characterization of autism as a clear 'problem.'

With all of this in mind, it is clear that we need to revise some of the 'facts' surrounding autism and its diagnosis. First, we have to admit that the diagnostic processes themselves produce an evaluative account of autism, one that makes clear assumptions about the individual experience of the condition. Equally, we need to see that these assumptions come to form a *narrative* of how autism is understood to affect people, a story that moves from presumptions about what the condition is, where it exists, and how it manifests itself, to what that then means for anyone to whom the label 'autistic' is applied. The 'fact' of such a storyline often leads to substantial consequences in the lives of those with autism, in terms of the ways they are seen by others, whether these be professionals involved in health or caring capacities, or the wider public. We also need to look in detail at the specific features of this narrative, so that we might comprehend the manner in which individual lives are affected. If we accept that, in part, diagnosis produces the 'person with autism,' we still have to return to the question of what kind of personhood—what humanity, what interiority, what socialized subject—might this obscure?

4 Intervention and Treatment

Metaphors, Objects, and Subjects

Given that autism is a spectrum condition, and because therefore we might say that there are many autisms, it is difficult to generalize about the ways in which it is experienced. Once a diagnosis has been arrived at, much of the subsequent attention from healthcare officials focuses on the range of social communication and interaction evident in individuals with the condition, and especially around the areas of behavior, intervention, and treatment. Here too, however, what might constitute a fact is a tricky and ambiguous area. In her comprehensive account of autism, taken from her own clinical and research experience, psychologist Laura Schreibman starts her chapter on treatments with the following observation: "Nowhere is controversy more evident in the field of autism than in the area of treatment. Here we even have controversies *within* controversies. The history of therapeutic interventions for this population is at once fascinating, depressing and hopeful" (Schreibman 2005, 133). I will detail the controversies Schreibman mentions here in Part III of this book, but for now we can see from this extract that the variables we have already noted in our discussion of what autism is thought to be inevitably map on to the ways in which it is then encountered in the world. Autism produces an often dizzying set of responses, from fascination and concern to sentimentality and fear, and those who seek to engage with this, or treat it, do so from multiple perspectives.

At the same time, it is wrong to think that the person with autism is simply a figure viewed from the outside, as much of the discussion so far in this section might imply, and a logic that is arguably still discernable in Schreibman's distancing phrase "this population." One of the most dominant facts about autism to have emerged in recent years is the way in which those who are autistic have challenged the degree to which they are only objects in the thoughts of others. As we shall see in Part II, more than ever before people with autism are vocal and articulate about their own histories and about the history of autism that came before them. Equally, there are more autistic communities than there have ever been, gathering together like-minded individuals (predominantly through the internet) who support one another, share experiences, and often advocate against what they perceive as prejudice and misrepresentation.

For these kinds of communities, it is often the issues surrounding intervention and treatment that produce most questions and commentary. As is the case for most disabilities, the history of care of those with autism—especially institutionalized care—is one full of misperceptions about the condition and, in its worst excesses, one of abuse. For much of the twentieth century, a central 'fact' about autism was the presumption that those who were autistic could not be treated and had nothing to offer society. As a consequence they were kept locked away, often in conditions of serious deprivation, and autism itself was equally hidden from mainstream society. In truth, it is only in the last two decades (and thus we should speak of a single generation) that those with autism have been freed from this presumptive 'knowledge,' and one result of this is that there are strong opinions about treatment and care from within autism communities and, frequently, their families. As might be expected, feelings run extremely high on this topic.

Following on from the logic that guides diagnosis, many of the ideas that underpin contemporary treatments of autism stem from a foundational notion of deficit. Most treatment methods focus on behavior, and in turn the majority of treatment methods based on behavior seek to counteract what are understood to be impairments. The 'triad of impairments,' the idea that the core of autistic behavior can be understood in terms of deficits of three central concepts—communication, imagination, and social interaction—is a highly influential paradigm for the discussion of autism that originated in the late 1970s and has dominated much thinking about the condition since (Wing and Gould 1979). At heart, the triad concerns questions of *processing*, the ways in which those with autism seek to make sense and respond to the world around them. Because, the logic goes, the brains of autistic individuals process experiences differently, they then struggle with the consequences of such processing—speech and communicating, understanding and generalizing, imagining outcomes etc. The component parts of the triad have themselves led to a number of other significant foundational ideas about autistic behavior, such as the belief that those with autism are 'mindblind,' or don't possess a 'theory of mind' that allows them to understand the perspectives and points of view of other people (Baron-Cohen 1995). In another influential extension of the triad, one that in fact seeks to bring its component parts together, it has been suggested that those with autism have "weak central coherence" (Biklen 2005, 40; Frith 2008, 90–94); in other words that they cannot process—or indeed do not see the need to—differences in a manner that makes them cohere into a general pattern. A third, and related, idea of such processing, which posits the notion that individuals who are autistic are unable to plan sequences and actions, to move from one step of any process to the next, is called 'executive function.' Like the theory of mind and central coherence theories, executive function has suggested forms that treatment of the condition might take, because in seeking to define the nature of the impairment, it makes clear possible actions that might compensate for this (Russell 1997).

Before we come to look at those treatments, we might dwell on the fact that, as Douglas Biklen has observed, the above processes that have developed from the 'triad of impairments' hypothesis all work as metaphors. The notion that ill health frequently functions in terms of metaphor has been most famously explored by Susan Sontag in her discussion of cancer, tuberculosis, and AIDS (Sontag 1991). For Sontag, illness is commonly a "metaphor for mortality, for human frailty and vulnerability," and health conditions described in metaphorical terms are "so overlaid with mystification" and "so much a vehicle for the large insufficiencies of [modern] culture" that they arguably function more in cultural terms than medical (Sontag 1991, 94 and 87). At present, autism operates precisely in the manner Sontag lays out; what was true of tuberculosis as the nineteenth century turned into the twentieth, that it was bound up in social narrative concerns of the era, is now true of autism as the twentieth has turned into the twenty-first. Biklen has noted that metaphor is ubiquitous when thinking about autism, that it often "operates as reality" (Biklen 2005, 37), and that the various processing metaphors outlined above actually all work in service of another, grander, metaphorical association, namely what he terms "autism-inside-the-person" (Biklen 2005, 37). This notion connects back to some of the medical research issues discussed earlier, and the idea of *where* autism is. The belief that individuals host or contain their autism, whether in a process that is benevolent or malevolent, is very powerful and is—again—possibly something that needs to be more understood as a cultural narrative rather than one that is medical or psychological. It appears to make sense, especially given the lack of any biological marker that might define the condition, and as a result it offers what seems to be a natural and intelligible explanation about autism's origins. At the same time, it leads to the proliferation of other metaphors about how autism should be treated, namely that, if the hosting is seen to be problematic, it requires a 'breakthrough' to release the person 'imprisoned,' or 'locked-in' by the condition. The suggestion that autism is a 'veil' or 'mask' that somehow hides a non-autistic person is one that, for all its lack of medical support, has had a considerable effect on the way many see the condition.

We are now, obviously, a long way from a certain kind of fact. There is little evidence here of the peer reviewed and verifiable scientific or medical study, put together over time and with appropriate controls. Rather, all issues surrounding the intervention and treatment of autism return us squarely to the terrain of what we *don't* know, even if we can see that they may have their origins in theories produced by developmental psychology. The metaphorical associations that surround treatment are evidence of how the lack of definitive knowledge of the condition invites suggestion and conjecture, and it is the realization that these are the most common frames for considering intervention when it comes to autism that should stand as the central fact about treatment. There is a lot of educated guesswork around, and much that is not educated at all. To pick up on the title of Paul Collins' 2004 book on autism, inspired by his son's condition, a significant amount of thinking about autism treatment is "not even wrong" (Collins 2004).

Behavior therapy and modification for those with autism began in the 1960s as a search to find practical methods, taken from psychological principles, which could overcome the perceived limitations displayed by those with autism. At heart, these processes were simple— behavior considered productive was rewarded, while that which was not deemed positive was ignored and went unrewarded. Such work, especially that undertaken in Los Angeles by Ivar Lovaas and James Simmons, challenged the assumption that autism was psychogenic in origin and should be treated from within a psychodynamic model. It also produced what were seen to be considerable breakthroughs. The behavior and social interaction of children with severe autism, institutionalized and in many cases subject to physical restraint for most of their lives, was observed to improve; some who had been non-verbal even learned the beginnings of speech. But the controversies caused by the techniques employed by Lovaas and Simmons were equally intense.

They were explicit about their use of 'pain and punishment as treatment techniques' (as the title of their co-authored 1969 article on their research put it). The children in the research programs at Lovaas and Simmons' Neuropsychiatric Institute at UCLA were verbally abused, often being shouted and screamed at when they failed to complete desired tasks. They were also restrained, shaken, slapped, and, in some cases, subjected to electric shock, all actions constituted as "negative reinforcers or aversive stimuli" (Lovaas and Simmons 1969, 23) and employed in efforts to modify their behavior.

Lovaas and Simmons' methods have cast a long shadow over the history of autism treatments. That they abused the children in their care is beyond question; condemnation of their techniques was voiced as they published their research in the late 1960s and grew in the decades that followed, especially from those within autism and other disability communities. The brutality of the methods, it was claimed, was justified by the fact that the shock induced in the children prompted them into an engagement with the research teams in ways that were otherwise impossible. Opponents argued that any form of violent treatment was more likely to result in violent responses and the internalization of violent behavior, although in response to this Lovaas and Simmons countered that psychodynamic treatments prior to their own work (which focused on issues of ego differentiation and parent/child relationships for example) often saw increases in such behaviors as self harming and violent outbursts when these were supposedly the very issues that such treatment was trying to reduce. Seen in hindsight, and in terms of balance, it is clear that Lovaas was wrong, and that his 1960s method was not as successful as he claimed; and even as he continued to stress the high number of children whose 'performance' improved through the use of behavioral therapy in his later research he also moved away from the recommendation of such "aversion techniques" (Lovaas 1987). At the same time, various behavioral approaches that would develop to make a real difference in the lives of people with autism had their source in this idea of treatment. As ever with autism, the picture is complex.

By the 1970s, it was clear that *some* form of behavioral therapy was likely to be the form of intervention that would prove most effective in working with autistic children. Further research following up treatment methods that began in California have developed into the one autism treatment model—Applied Behavior Analysis, or ABA—that, as Schreibman has noted, "has been empirically demonstrated to be effective for children with autism" (Schreibman 2005, 133). ABA, which is compromised of an intensive series of one-to-one teaching sessions based around the 'reward' idea, has become one of the most used methods of intervention with autistic children, and extensive studies have corroborated its effectiveness in producing positive developments in young children's learning. Because of its emphasis on a one-to-one learning style however, it is not always easily accommodated within school systems, though some schools do implement a version of it. It is also the case that the required intensity (often 40 hours a week of close work is deemed necessary) can make it prohibitively expensive for many families, since it requires either the employment of a trained teacher or that a parent undergoes training and gives up employment.

ABA can be seen to be the positive that has emerged from the problematic period of experimentation in behavioral therapy during the 1960s. Many children with autism benefit from the kind of early intervention that ABA provides, with its creation of a platform on which further learning can build, and the success of its structures and methods mark it out as being clearly distinct from a number of other methods of behavioral intervention. At the same time, this does not remove the question surrounding whether autism itself is a condition that requires 'treatment' per se. Various ongoing ideas about the integrity of autistic lives and the ways in which aspects of the condition can be reconstituted in a positive light challenge the logic that 'deficit requires correction.' As with previous points made in this section about medical research, when it comes to many forms of intervention and treatment we find ourselves back with the uncomfortable truth that the most informative fact about the whole area may be the need to admit to what we don't know. The often dizzying array of such treatments—from drug regimes that purport to balance chemical and mineral levels in the body, to spiritualist conceptions of autism that connect it to pre-modern ideas of self and lost narratives of knowledge—are bewildering. We shall return to think through a number of these in Part III of this book, especially with connection to the controversial issue of arguments surrounding 'curing' autism, but it is worthwhile stressing here that such treatments

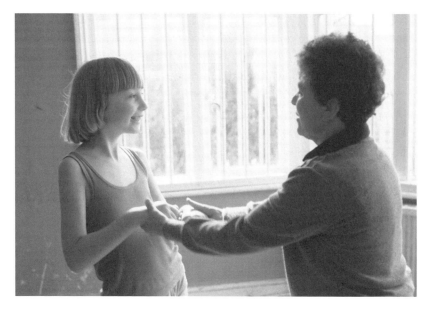

Figure 1.5 Autistic girl with therapist
© Anthea Sieveking/Wellcome Images

can only exist in the absence of any consensus concerning the question of intervention. Children with autism have inadvertently been killed during religious exorcisms and as a result of speculative pharmaceutical intervention, all in the name of 'treatment.' When events such as these take place—when it is thought that there can be a logic for attempting such 'corrections'—we should recognize that we are far from an appropriate understanding of how we should structure our encounters with autism.

5 The Gender Question and the Nature of Being

One of the most repeated facts about autism revolves around gender, namely that diagnosis reveals that it is a predominantly male condition, with a ratio of approximately 4:1 in favor of male over female cases.

The clarity of such a statistic has led to the conclusion that there might be something *inherently* male about autism, and that part of understanding what it is and how it works can come from thinking through questions of masculinity. In many ways the source for this line of thought is the earliest clinical work on the condition that took place in the 1940s. I will detail this history more thoroughly in Part II, but it is worth noting here that in his 1944 research paper on autism, written following the observation of a number of children in his clinic, Hans Asperger declared that: "The autistic personality is an extreme variant of male intelligence . . . In the autistic individual, the male pattern is exaggerated to the extreme" (Asperger 1991, 84–85). This logic has informed much work on autism in the decades that have followed; in his 2003 study *The Essential Difference: Men, Women and the Extreme Male Brian*, Simon Baron-Cohen notes that "the male brain is predominantly hard-wired for understanding and building systems," and cites this in contrast to the female brain, which he characterizes as being more reliant on empathy (Baron-Cohen 2003, 1).

The details of the 'extreme maleness' theory are easy to recognize. The variety of 'special abilities' that some individuals with autism possess, skills associated with memorization or calculation for example, are exactly the kind of 'systematizing' processes identified by Baron-Cohen. The general cultural knowledge we have and share about autism reinforces this view, in our assumptions that those with autism are good at math, or obsessed with statistics or objects. These are seen to be extensions, or Asperger's 'exaggerations,' of the kinds of activities that boys and men undertake because they 'naturally' find them interesting. To pick one possible case study of how such logic can be pursued: where is the boundary between a 'normal' collection of baseball cards and an obsessive one that might, to some, suggest autism? Interestingly, we sometimes frame this kind of question in terms of talking about a 'healthy' level of interest, leaving its alternative and opposite—the 'unhealthy'—unspoken. Equally, where does the geek or nerd adolescent, obsessed with technology, stand in relation to such questions, or the adult 'trainspotter,' a British byword for restricted interests that are held to be innately male?

In part, these questions return us to the neurobiological and genetic, since it is clear that the kind of research discussed earlier, which looks at the structure of the brain or genetic inheritance, can also accommodate the inclusion of gender as a meaningful variable. Studies on levels of fetal testosterone, or work that examines autism in the light of other neurobehavioral conditions that have gender differentials in their genetic patterning, offer suggestive possibilities about links between the condition and masculinity. Even given some of the reservations about diagnostic processes that were discussed previously, the stark disparity in the gender breakdown of those diagnosed and the linkage to questions of connectivity in male and female brains mean that conceiving autism within the frame of gender difference is a necessary avenue for research.

At the same time, the idea of the condition being an 'extreme' kind of masculinity does potentially push thinking about autism into (ironically) some restricted areas. Many of the most well-known figures with autism are male—Kim Peek, the main model for Dustin Hoffman's character in Barry Levinson's 1988 film *Rain Man*, is probably the most obvious—but the most heralded writers with the condition are all female. Temple Grandin, Donna Williams, and Dawn Prince-Hughes are individuals whose work has made it possible for a majority audience to approach and understand the interiority of autistic lives, and while it can be argued that Grandin's descriptions of her autism fit the kind of systematizing central to Baron-Cohen's theories, the same is not true of Williams, whose autobiographies reveal a much more impressionistic and sensory-based response to the world (Williams 1992). Indeed, recognition of the importance of such sensory experiences should be considered a fact of autism as much as that evidence provided by narrow interests and restricted or obsessive patterns of behavior. Autism is as often encountered in terms of a response to light, textures, and sounds as it is seen in a love of railway timetables or computer games, and although this is mentioned in passing in diagnostic manuals such as the *DSM* and *ICD*, it receives limited focus.

Equally, there are numerous instances of autism in males that do not correspond to systematizing tendencies, and indeed there are examples of patterning or systems that we can understand as not being about repetition or restriction. The world of visual arts is revealing here: the artist Larry Bissonnette was diagnosed with schizophrenia before his autism was recognized, and he learned to draw when he was a non-verbal child. His paintings, which he often makes with his hands, are frequently long rectangles on which urban or suburban housing scenes are juxtaposed with some element of his own presence, either his name or, in some cases, a Polaroid photograph of himself (see Figure 1.6).

Bissonnette's paintings do not conform to the more established forms of autistic art, such as that practiced by Stephen Wiltshire, in which extraordinary feats of memorization are reproduced quickly and in great technical detail (see Figure 1.7). Rather, Bissonnette's work presents recognizable but abstracted scenes in which he places traces of himself into the world of the paintings. The results are not structured around systems of memory, as with Wiltshire, but are rather different patterns of creativity in which Bissonnette figures himself, the creator but also the person with autism, as a central element.

And where systematized patterns do occur in art they do not have to be seen in terms of limits. Although never diagnosed, Andy Warhol easily fitted many of the criteria that are now used to determine Asperger's Syndrome, especially in terms of obsessive and patterned behavior. In his art, of course, such patterning was explored to an extent that changed the nature of twentieth-century painting. If we agree that Warhol's paintings are 'repetitious' to any degree, and if we allow ourselves to see him within a frame of masculine autistic creativity, then it is clear that the repetition is by no means a deficit. As part of Pop Art's renegotiation of the idea of the artwork and examination of consumer culture, Warhol's 'restrictions' are in fact highly significant cultural statements.

Figure 1.6 Larry Bissonnette, *Goaline Stance of Larry's Signature Obliterates Ordered Land of Slated Houses*

© GRACE gallery

Figure 1.7 Stephen Wiltshire, *Chicago Street Scene*
© The Stephen Wiltshire Gallery

Autism and gender remains a contested field, and as such is in fact part of wider arguments about the relationship between science and gender. For all the relevance of the points made above concerning autism and masculinity, the notion that males function as systematizers and women as empathizers is far from being accepted by those within the scientific research community. It is clear that research into the interplay between autism and gender, especially in the context of genetics, is still imperative and may well provide vital information concerning the nature of the condition. It is also clear, though, that there are problematic stereotypes that can emerge from an over-simplistic adherence to the unsubstantiated 'fact' of 'extreme maleness.' There is, however, another consideration that comes from the question of whether men or women are somehow 'more' or 'less' autistic than one another, namely the notion that, transcending gender, autism is in some way a form of proof of a general humanity. Because of its status as a spectrum condition, autism is recognized as existing in many forms, and the possibility that this allows for the suggestion that we are 'all a little bit autistic' is readily apparent. The various meanings of such a statement are more complicated than they might appear though; they indicate both a positive outcome because of the opportunity to normalize autism through an association with general human variation, but also a potential stretching of the category 'autistic' to a point where it may be useless. Indeed, this last point, although it might originate from a position that seeks to be sympathetic, may well create problems for those who do have autism precisely because it removes much of the specificity about what the condition actually is.

So where does this leave us when trying to speak of connections between autism and an idea of 'the human'? We will look at this more fully in Part III, but certainly to discuss autism in any way is to necessarily engage with core questions of what constitutes humanity. As Paul Collins observes, there is a potential irony in this given that many people, including many who have autism, think of the condition in terms of it being an 'alien' subjectivity. Collins summarizes the position nicely:

> Autists are described by others—and by themselves—as aliens among humans. But there's an irony to this, for precisely the opposite is true. They are us, and to understand them is to begin to understand what it means to be human. Think of it: a disability is usually defined in terms of what is missing . . . But autism is *an ability and a disability*: it is as much about what is abundant as what is missing, an overexpression of the very traits that make our species unique. Other animals are social, but only

humans are capable of abstract logic. The autistic outhumans the humans, and we can scarcely recognize the result.

(Collins 2004, 161, emphasis in original)

If, for Collins, autism represents an abundance of humanity, for other writers disability conditions in general point to a constructive idea of the *post*-human, precisely because the difference that comes with disability works as a reminder that there is not any shared singular condition of 'the human.' In truth, and despite the seeming disparity in the nomenclature, both positions have much in common. Collins' idea of 'outhuman[ing] the humans' is, as the phrasing makes apparent, a version of the post-human argument, and the kind of critique that it contains fits with the wider post-human position on disability. Certainly autism works in this way, as a vantage point from within which the range of humanity can be viewed. To say this, however, is not to say that there is an easy way we can all identify some form of autism within ourselves; possibly Collins' statement that we can 'scarcely recognize' the consequences of thinking about autism and the human is one to highlight in this regard—it is another version of our admitting to what we don't know. That autistic difference highlights human difference *is* a fact however, and one that is best understood in positive terms. Those with autism are not somehow inevitably 'other,' or fundamentally separated from those without the condition, and there is much to know and learn by thinking about the connections between the various versions of humanity to which autism provides a lens.

6 Conclusion

After the Fact

Autism is not an illness. Though it can sometimes be associated with serious health complications, especially connected to seizure disorders and issues relating to diet and nutrition, it is not in and of itself a condition that produces ill health. This is a fact that is worth under-scoring, and one sometimes lost in the labeling of the condition as a 'disease,' something that often accompanies discussion of autism in both medical and public arenas. The popular lexicon easily embraces the notion that it is possible for any individual to have something 'wrong' with them, and the baggy nature of this word allows for the easy crossover between illness and a neurobehavioral condition such as autism. Easy as it might be, however, we should resist such simplifica-tions given that they misrepresent and obscure far more than they reveal. Those with autism may well visit their doctor far less frequently than those without. They may not 'suffer' at all. Their health may be fine.

This journey through the 'facts' of autism has possibly served to muddy the waters, and arguably has made things less clear than might have been anticipated at the outset of our investigation. This is something neither expected nor desired when the facts of any given medical condition are laid out, a situation in which clarity is crucial. In terms of definitions and assessment, or diagnosis and treatment, it seems that there is little about autism on which there is universal acceptance. And yet there is a real value in pointing this out as a fact in itself. It helps in our understanding of what autism is if we know that the lack of scientific or medical consensus suggests that it is more than a single entity, or has multiple triggers and manifestations. Equally, it helps to see that the thinking that frequently passes for knowledge or fact is often narrativized and characterizes both the condition and those who have it in certain distinct ways. This is knowledge in its own right. To understand more about autism, to bring more viewpoints to bear on how we have come to see it in the ways in which we have, we need to move beyond the facts to deal with the multiple stories it produces and through which it is in turn produced. Central to this is the history of the condition itself, and it is to this that we now turn in Part II.

PART II
SOCIAL, CULTURAL, AND POLITICAL HISTORIES

7 Autism before Modern Medicine

In a very real sense, the history of autism is a recent one. The word 'autism' comes from the Greek *autos*, meaning self, and was first used by Eugen Bleuler in 1908, subsequently appearing in his published work in 1911. Bleuler was a Swiss psychiatrist who also coined the term 'schizophrenia,' and his understanding of autism was not as we would recognize it today but rather as a kind of non-logical thought that formed part of his wider research around the emerging ideas of dementia and the schizophrenic mind. Autism as we currently understand it dates from the late 1930s and early 1940s and the work of psychiatrists Leo Kanner and Hans Asperger who, independently of one another and on different continents, used the word to describe some of the children they studied in their own clinical research.

Adam Feinstein begins his 2010 study *A History of Autism*, the first book of its kind, by discussing the work of Kanner and Asperger, and the two men are rightly seen as being foundational in the study of what we consider the condition to be. But if we acknowledge that current research has established autism as being neurobiological and part of the general pattern of human variation, we also need to concede that this will have always been the case. As a result, individuals with autism have always been part of the fabric of humanity, and have been members of all societies and cultures before the twentieth century. Is it then possible to talk about autism before it had a medical formulation? What would it look like and how might we recognize it? The terminology that has made the condition visible is very contemporary, so how would the linguistic and narrative conventions that pre-date these possibly suggest any idea of autistic presence?

These are questions that necessarily invite guesswork. Writers on autism have identified case studies from the past in which individuals have been described in terms that seem, to our eyes and with our knowledge, to suggest that they had the condition. Probably the two best-known examples of this are Victor, the so-called 'Wild Boy of Aveyron,' a non-verbal feral child found in forests in central France in 1797, and Kaspar Hauser, a teenager who suddenly appeared on the streets of Nuremberg in Germany in 1828 with documentation that suggested he had spent all his life up to that point enclosed in a basement dungeon. Both cases were widely discussed in their time, not least because of the ways in which they fed easily into Enlightenment debates concerning the potential 'natural' dimension of human nature. In her 1989 study *Autism: Explaining the Enigma*, Uta Frith concludes that, while it is quite possible that Victor did indeed have autism, a claim she makes based on a reading of impairments in his social and imaginative abilities, Kaspar Hauser, who was far more linguistically able, probably did not (Frith 1989, 16–33). At heart, opinions such as those professed by Frith are based on an extension of the theory of the triad of impairments back into whatever records still exist about the children in question.

Frith expands her study to include more generic speculation, discussing metaphors of distancing and lack of connection in European fairy tales, and the reports of Russian 'Blessed Fools,' individuals who, from the sixteenth to the nineteenth centuries, were known for their social eccentricity and obsessive behaviors and often lived on the outskirts of settlements where locals read their isolation in terms of religious devotion (Frith 1989, 36–40). Certainly the most sensible way to locate autism in any pre-medical manifestation is to try to view it in this way through the logic of the cultural and linguistic systems of the time, and the widespread notion of 'the fool,' especially thought of in terms of expansive language and stereotypical or repetitive behaviors, allows for the possibility of a glimpse into what autism might have been.

The suggestiveness inherent in retrospective 'diagnosis' has made it an obvious attraction because of its appeal as a form of mystery, and one noteworthy trend in recent writing on the condition has been a process of 'outing' historical figures. In a manner that is possibly explicable given the idea that autism is a systematizing condition, figures in the fields of science, math, and philosophy, from Isaac Newton and Albert Einstein to Ludwig Wittgenstein and Alan Turing, have had both their work and lives re-read in terms of their supposed autism, often being elevated to the status of 'autism heroes.' In the arts, the tendency has been even more widespread, and publications have speculated on the autistic tendencies of a range of writers. Henry Thoreau, Herman Melville, Emily Dickinson, Lewis Carroll, Hans Christian Anderson, Sherwood Anderson, W.H. Auden, and George Orwell have all been suggested as being on the spectrum, and at least three books have been written on the topic of autism and artistic creativity. In terms of fictional characters who might be autistic or have Asperger's Syndrome, claims have been made for figures in the work of William Wordsworth, Herman Melville, Charles Dickens, Joseph Conrad, Arthur Conan Doyle, and William Faulkner (Brown 2010; Fitzgerald 2004; Fitzgerald 2005).

The issues involved in talking about autism before the middle of the twentieth century are clearly complex. The lack of consensus surrounding the origins and forms of the condition, as established in Part I, are obviously multiplied many times over when it comes to the consideration of time periods that lack any kind of specific clinical definition. Anything and everything can, it seems, be seen to be autistic: slight behavioral traits discovered in letters or written accounts can be seized upon as proof; anecdotal information remembered by acquaintances is disproportionately elevated to the status of informed knowledge; and the idea of impairment associated with the condition means that even the absence of facts (in terms of, say, an individual not especially good at 'social interaction') can be interpreted as evidence. The potential for a fictionalization of the past is obvious here, and seems not to have any clear-cut boundaries. In fact, such speculation is probably best seen not as a desire to engage with autism in the historical record, but rather as a peculiarly *contemporary* fascination with neurobehavioral difference in which we look for the condition everywhere. And to search endlessly for autism in the past is, in some ways, still a point about searching for definitions of it in the present, still a comment about what we don't know.

At the same time the central fact remains: there have been people with autism before the twentieth-century medical codifications of the condition came into effect, and we are not wrong to want to find traces of such presence where we can because, in doing so, we might potentially fill in some of the gaps in our understanding. In effect, this problem becomes an extended version of that discussed in Part I of this book, namely how to navigate between the tensions of what knowledge about autism is perceived to be, but one in which even less of the terrain is secure. In part, the simple assertion that autism did not only come into existence in the twentieth century (although, as we shall see, the ways in which this process took place has undoubtedly shaped how the condition is understood) is itself a useful challenge to a limited comprehension. But it is clearly the case that any kind of claim concerning the long history of autism needs to be made with real expertise, and not left to excited or over-eager guesswork.

One area where we are on slightly more stable ground is the interaction between autism and the nineteenth-century outlining of the 'idiot' figure. Here, it is probably wrong to talk of an 'autism before modern medicine'; rather we should see this period as a transitional zone in which developing medical ideas of the mind and behavior began to take the forms that would allow for the kinds of specialization in psychiatry that saw the later specific identification of the condition. The links between the two words are undeniable—even 10 to 15 years ago the term 'idiot savant' was not an uncommon term used to describe some people with autism—but 'idiocy' does not have, and never did have, any clear diagnostic outline. Rather, in the words of Martin Halliwell, who has written a cultural history of the topic, it functioned as "a symbolical repository for that which defies categorization" (Halliwell 2004, 5). An increasingly common term from the mid-nineteenth century onwards, idiocy was a product of the increased levels of institutionalization and monitoring of the period, a time when economic and social determinants drove new forms of classification.

It received high-profile coverage in studies such as Edouard Séguin's 1866 *Idiocy and Its Treatment by the Physiological Method*, which began to differentiate it from the larger category of madness. In the ways in which idiocy developed as a distinct manifestation of intellectual impairment, we can see how it heralded ideas that would become part of later definitions of autism. Halliwell cites an 1897 account of 'the idiot' by Frederic Bateman, a Fellow of the Royal College of Physicians, in which he observes the following:

> An idiot is a human being who possesses the tripartite nature of man—body, soul and spirit . . . but who is the subject of an infirmity consisting, anatomically, of a defective organization and want of development of the brain, resulting in an inability, more or less complete, for the exercise of the intellectual, moral and sensitive faculties.
>
> (Halliwell 2004, 9–10)

Though this is very much the prose of its time, we can see how it could lead, as the twentieth century progressed, to a more sure-footed medicalized idea of autism. Bateman's highlighting of the working of the brain would, gradually, overtake the emphasis on 'moral faculties' as time progressed. The 'tripartite nature' of body, soul, and spirit, a favorite idea in the nineteenth century, would be transformed into the more recognizably medical notion of the 'cognitive' as idiocy was replaced by other technical terms. Here, we can surmise that the idiot may well be the person with autism, and that in terms of diagnosis and medical research aspects of 'idiocy' are indeed autism as understood by the clinical language of the period.

The idiot and the individual with autism can be seen, if we work through the prose of the later nineteenth century in identifying the former and seek to anticipate the emerging shapes of the latter, to have potential overlaps. Ideas of isolation, of restrictions with regard to language and communication, and of imagination can be found in accounts, both scientific and fictional, that describe people with each label. In Joseph Conrad's story 'The Idiots' for example, written in 1896 and published in the 1898 collection *Tales of Unrest*, a French peasant couple have four children, the 'idiots' of the title, each of which has a severe intellectual

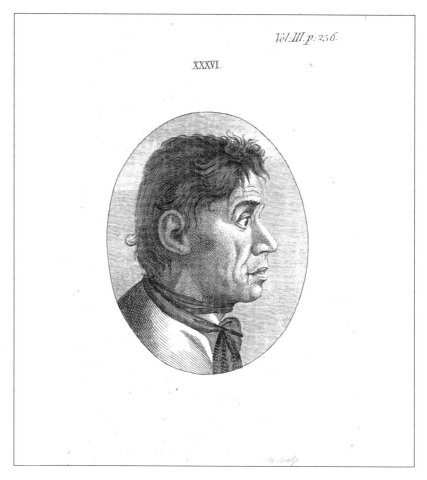

Figure 2.1 *Profile view of idiot man,* from Lavater's *Essays on Physiognomy* (1789–98)
© Wellcome Library, London

impairment. The description of the third child, shortly after birth, displays the kind of language that would come to be used in case studies of young children with autism some 60 years later:

> That child, like the other two, never smiled, never stretched its hand to her [mother], never spoke, never had a glance of recognition for her in its big black eyes which could stare fixedly at any glitter, but failed hopelessly to follow the brilliance of a sun-ray slipping slowly along the floor.
>
> (Conrad 1898, 92)

Here, the avoidance of contact with a parent (especially eye contact) and the potential obsession inherent in the 'stare' at the 'glitter' do indeed sound like some forms of what is still called early infantile autism. For Conrad to be able to produce such representations there must have been a common cultural currency in which individuals with neurobehavioral conditions were recognized, discussed, and judged.

We can say with some confidence that a number of people classed as idiots in the nineteenth century would have had autism. There is enough of an evidential and representational link for us to be able to justify such a statement. The link between the two terms remains imprecise, and the slippage that necessarily exists because of different formations and nomenclatures produces a space that is not easy to bridge (and, of course, this is even more the case when we look further back through history). But individuals with autism were part of the fabric of earlier societies, even if we can only dimly imagine or chart their lives. Such imagination becomes easier as the nineteenth turns into the twentieth century and the outlining of intellectual disabilities becomes more technical and nuanced. To understand the ways in which autism emerges from this process, we need to explore its link to the developing nature of psychiatry during the period.

8 The Development of Child Psychiatry

Kanner and Asperger

One productive way to think of the rise of psychiatry during the nineteenth century is to see it as a product of a medical desire to differentiate and specialize. As medical models of the body and mind gathered empirical characteristics, the biological notion of the 'feeble-minded' developed to accompany other newly outlined categories, such as the 'degenerate' and 'deviant' (and indeed that of the 'idiot'), which extended and complicated earlier ideas of 'madness.' As these terms suggest, much of the point of such vocabularies was to articulate processes of social control, and the links between 'mental deficiency' and criminality were ever present. A notable by-product of such a desire for control was the development of the asylum as a space of separation, a site where those with cognitive difference were sequestered in the name of a greater social good. But the asylum also became a space of study, as 'confinement' allowed for detailed examination of those inside. More than ever before, doctors now had the opportunity to observe and to refine their diagnostic criteria. The nineteenth-century asylum was many things, but one of these was a laboratory for psychiatric research.

This research produced all manner of conclusions. Psychosis, neurosis, psychopathology, and personality disorder were all terms refined as the century ended, with Sigmund Freud's work being pivotal in the new formations. And, accompanying this, a gradual process of age differentiation saw increasing research into 'insanity' in children. For the most part, children were not admitted into asylums, but those that were (often those with the most visible disabilities) became, like their adult counterparts, subjects for observation. Henry Maudsley wrote a chapter on childhood psychosis in a medical textbook published in 1879, and the category of the 'idiot child' became established as one in its own right during the period. In the early decades of the twentieth century, a combination of medical, social, and educational concerns produced a new focus on children with disabilities, and new kinds of specialization—pediatrics, child psychology, and child psychiatry among them—produced doctors who focused exclusively on childhood conditions. With the accompanying shift from the asylum to the medical clinic, a movement that occurred in response to social concerns, children were in the medical research spotlight as never before.

Such developments explain the career of a figure such as Leo Kanner, who came to publish a succession of foundational articles outlining autism in the mid-twentieth century. Kanner was exactly this kind of child psychiatry specialist: his *Child Psychiatry*, published in 1935, was the first English language textbook on the subject and the clinic in which he worked at Johns Hopkins Hospital in Baltimore, itself the first child psychiatric clinic at any teaching hospital in the world, brought to bear all the latest research on the issues of children,

Figure 2.2 Autistic boy looking out of window. What Leo Kanner characterized as 'aloneness' may involve a different sensory perception of the world

© Anthea Sieveking/Wellcome Images

disability, and mental health. Many of the initial 'facts' outlining autism come from the pioneering study of 11 children in Kanner's clinic that he published in 1943, in an article entitled 'Autistic Disturbances of Affective Contact.'

For Kanner, 'affective contact' meant meaningful interaction with others, and the absence of this was one of the key characteristics he indentified in the children he observed. In addition, he stressed that the children displayed a marked and "anxious" desire for the "preservation of sameness," as he put it, especially in terms of wanting to maintain regular routines and their responses to their surroundings. They also had very little language, and that which they did possess appeared not to be directed towards personal communication. Kanner also noted that the children exhibited a fascination with objects, which they would use in obsessive ways that differed from other children of the same ages. Interestingly, in a move that subsequent researchers would come to challenge, Kanner asserted that the children he worked with were not intellectually 'retarded,' but rather of average to above-average intelligence, since their performance in certain tests connected to memory and spatial organization was often impressive. In summing up these observations in a phrase which sought to combine them all, Kanner concluded that the condition he was describing was characterized by "extreme autistic aloneness" (Kanner 1943, 242).

Kanner's perception saw a pattern, a unique "pure culture example" of a condition as he termed it in his paper, which had not been identified before (Kanner 1943, 245). Over the next few decades his outline of autism would come to be seen as being foundational in subsequent research, and the term 'Kanner's autism,' or 'classic autism,' was coined to describe those young children who seemed most 'obviously' autistic in the ways that they conformed to the central aspects of his findings. In many ways then, Kanner's establishing of the criteria for diagnosis created the template for the identification of the child with autism, the figure we might pluck from our memory or imagination today—the mute or echolalic, hand-flapping, self-stimulating child. Remembering our exploration of the workings of diagnosis in Part I of this book however, we can see that it is a particular type of narrative construction that allowed such a process to take place. Part of this narrative is the general development of medical research that produced Kanner as the kind of expert he was, but part of it is also the logic he brought to bear in asserting his actual findings. 'Aloneness,' for example, is a term that may seem natural to describe the various actions Kanner witnessed in the children in the study, but it is also an evaluative word that invites conclusions about the emotional states of those individuals labeled in such a manner. Sue Rubin, a woman with autism, wrote a 2005 'conversation' with Kanner in which she critiqued precisely this aspect of his formulation in an interaction with his 1943 article. Although Rubin writes "being alone is sometimes my only sanctuary," she also observes that "an autistic person's degree of detachment varies." "What Kanner thought unusual," Rubin concludes in a comment that unveils the logic of the diagnostic method, "I find quite reasonable" (Biklen 2005, 90, 100, and 88).

Rubin's insider account of autism highlights the structure of Kanner's analytic method. Though it might seem inevitable that this would be the case, Kanner's methods of appraisal created *behavior* as the central determinant in how autism is constituted, and as Rubin notes, behavior outside of the clinic and in social settings is both relative but also always subject to judgment. This may seem to be a fussy point: given that there are no biological markers for autism, how else might the condition be identified if not through behavior? But we have seen in Part I the consequences of diagnosis performed in this manner, and the ways in which judgments on behavior can become so easily surrounded with language that stresses the negative. The actual conclusions to be drawn here are less about autism itself, and more about the authority of the medical researcher and the commentary provided on research subjects. As with many other disabilities, the clinical observation of autism was brought into being by the *process* of looking for it, one of voyeuristic authority, and then generalizing from the results subsequently found.

Kanner's testing and surveillance methodology also created two other aspects of autism that have come to dominate contemporary thought about the condition: first, and inevitably, it meant that autism came to be associated predominantly with children, and thus with a specific idea of child development; and second, the fact that the children in his clinic were objects of enquiry in the way that they were, that they were observed with a supposedly dispassionate and detached clinical gaze, stressed the ability of the expert to *read* the condition in the process of assessment. This returns us especially to the idea, mentioned in Part I, of autism being *hosted* by anyone who has it. As we saw there, Douglas Biklen has identified this as the "autism-inside-the person" model (Biklen 2005, 34), in which traits and behaviors are understood to be contained within the individual concerned, and the job of the psychiatrist is to unpack or unveil them during diagnosis. When seen in terms of metaphor, it is clear that this type of formulation has, in part, led to some of the many ideas popular in cultural narratives, especially that which asserts that autism somehow inhabits a body that is not autistic, and that the two might be prised apart in some way, with the non-autistic, 'real,' self saved from the disability. The many common metaphors of isolation, withdrawal, breakthroughs, and fortresses that accompany discussions of the condition stem from this kind of formation. And, in the wake of Susan Sontag's work on illness and metaphor discussed in Part I, we can further understand that the idea of autism being 'inside' the body also characterizes the condition *in and of itself*, as if it is a malignant presence and something separate, like a cancer or a demon spirit that requires removal. It is, of course, not fair to blame Kanner for the fact that such ideas about autism exist, but if part of our understanding of the condition involves plotting the trajectories that have led us to our contemporary conceptions, then we need to be clear-sighted about how such narratives have been formed.

With Kanner autism came into a certain kind of focus. Intriguingly, at the same time but thousands of miles away Hans Asperger was producing research that would come to shape the condition that now bears his name, a condition that overlaps but does not quite neatly fit autism as Kanner saw it. In his clinic in Vienna, Asperger observed four boys, aged between six and eleven, and also came to use the word 'autistic' to describe their behavior. There is debate about how the two figures worked in seeming ignorance of one another. Feinstein's recent history of autism has established that Asperger first lectured and published (in German) on the idea of 'autistic psychopathology' in 1938 (Feinstein 2010, 10), whereas it was previously believed that his first publication on the topic came in 1944, and so after that of Kanner. As a German speaker of Austrian extraction himself, Kanner would have had more reason than most medical researchers to know of Asperger's work, which had been ongoing throughout the 1930s, but there is no mention of it in his 1943 paper, nor in his subsequent follow-up research. It is probably not essential to establish exactly who knew what first—after all most 'originators' in research or technology turn out to have based their work on some similar version that pre-dates the moment of 'discovery'—but there is something highly suggestive in the notion that autism 'appears' in two places at once, as if it is a zeitgeist phenomenon or a condition just waiting to be identified at a particular moment in time.

Like Kanner, Asperger discussed impairments in social interaction in the children he observed, and also noted issues of obsession and compulsion, and of the threat posed by changes to environments and surroundings. He also, of course, reinforced the 'inside-the-person' model, given that, as an academic who came to work in a university clinic in Vienna in the 1940s, his analytical method mirrored that of Kanner. Asperger's children, however, displayed far greater linguistic range than those in Kanner's Baltimore study, and he claimed that his condition could not be recognized in infancy, unlike Kanner who noted that autism was usually discernable within the first 30 months.

Kanner's and Asperger's work dominated thinking about autism in the fields of psychiatry and social psychology in the decades following the 1940s. Though some have argued that autism and Asperger's Syndrome are distinct and separate, and indeed Asperger himself saw the condition he studied as a 'personality disorder' without the organic dimension identified in autism from early on in the research, most experts see the overlaps, rather than the differences, between the two conditions. Because much of Asperger's work was not translated into English until the 1980s, it was Kanner's findings in particular that guided thinking about autism, with his diagnostic criteria leading indirectly to the development of the 'triad of impairments' discussed in Part I of this book.

Undoubtedly, these were vital developments. However, for all the importance of such medical legacies, any account of the development of autism from the 1940s onwards needs to move beyond the idea that it was only the 'hero-doctor' involved in detailing the condition. The children analyzed by Kanner and Asperger, and the others who came in subsequent studies, might appear to be lost in the prose of the research article, or confined to notes in university archives, but of course they were at the beginning of their own complex lives and, as the first figures diagnosed with the condition, they should be seen as commanding a foundational position in the history of autism. Kanner's first subject in his 1943 article, his 'Case 1,' is referred to as 'Donald T.' Donald T is Donald Triplett, born in 1933 in Forest, Mississippi. Institutionalized in 1937 in his home state because of challenging behavior, Donald presented mannerisms that local doctors, who sought to understand him in terms of illness, were unable to comprehend, and when his parents took him back home in 1938 they were no closer to any kind of useful diagnosis. Donald's parents, who came from a financial background and so were relatively wealthy, contacted Kanner in Baltimore, and between 1938 and 1942 took Donald to the Johns Hopkins clinic on four separate occasions. As Kanner worked up the 11 case studies that would form the basis of his research, Donald was central to his emerging under-standing of autism. In Kanner's prose Donald emerges as the sum of his behaviors; he is described in this way:

He wandered about smiling, making stereotyped movements with his fingers, crossing them about in the air. He shook his head from side to side, whispering or humming the same three-note tune. He spun with great pleasure anything he could seize upon to spin. He kept throwing things on the floor, seeming to delight in the sounds they made. He arranged beads, sticks or blocks in different series of colors. Whenever he finished one of these performances, he squealed and jumped up and down. Beyond this he showed no initiative, requiring constant instruction (from his mother) in any form of activity other than the limited ones in which he was absorbed.

(Kanner 1943, 219)

Assessed in such terms, Donald's future beyond the Johns Hopkins clinic looked difficult if not downright bleak: a severely disabled child with a condition understood by no one beyond a few specialists. Kanner's article projects him into an uncertain life; of follow-up testing in which he will feature as a research subject, but with no sense that his subjectivity or inner life will be understood or accommodated.

In 2010, journalists from *The Atlantic* magazine, looking into the history of autism, found Donald, still living in Forest (Donovan and Zucker, 2010). Aged 77, he lives alone, although has close contact with his brother, who lives locally. Donald attended college in Jackson, majored in French, and sang in the college choir. He drives to his local golf club where he plays every day, and has become a keen, if not obsessive, traveler, having visited 28 states and 36 foreign countries since he began venturing abroad in his 30s. Part of the communal fabric in Forest, where he has been accepted ever since he was a child, Donald's life has been one that might not have seemed possible from the impressions given of him in Kanner's article. But that life is the inevitable counter-narrative to the medical account in which he is the original child with autism. For all of his status as the foundational research subject of the condition, such a 'fact' pales into insignificance when set against the detail and value of the life that Donald, and others like him, would go on to lead. While not all of Kanner or Asperger's children will have had lives such as Donald's, and we should be careful not to generalize from his experiences alone, he is nevertheless an example of a history of autism that puts other, clinical, accounts into context.

We should read Kanner, Asperger, and Donald Triplett equally as central figures in the mid-twentieth-century history of autism. But the psychiatric work of the first two, and the developing life of the latter, still left a crucial question unanswered: If the research of the 1940s helped to *identify* autism, it did little to suggest what *caused* the condition. A more systematic initial search for causes would come in the 1950s and 1960s, and would produce alarming results.

9 Psychoanalysis, Bruno Bettelheim, Parents, and Blame

Reading Leo Kanner's 1943 article now, it is impossible not to notice that one element of the children in his study appears to fascinate Kanner almost as much as the research subjects he was observing. This is the family stories, and especially the details of the parents of the children in his clinic. These stories form a distinct parallel narrative to that of the main research being undertaken. Kanner seems unable not to comment on the parents of the children he worked on, noticing that they were all "highly intelligent" for example, and that "there is a great deal of obsessiveness in the family background." He then went on to write six sentences that were to have a significant impact on the way autism was seen for the next 30 years:

> One other fact stands out predominantly. In the whole group, there are few really warmhearted fathers and mothers. For the most part, the parents, grandparents, and collaterals are persons strongly preoccupied with abstractions of a scientific, literary, or artistic nature, and limited in genuine interest in people. Even some of the happiest marriages are rather cold and formal affairs. Three of the marriages were dismal failures.

The question arises whether or to what extent this fact has contributed to the condition of the children.

(Kanner 1943, 250)

In both the first and last sentence here, this rather casual and subjective observation on Kanner's part is elevated to the status of 'fact,' and the suggestion posed by the insertion of this fact into the 'question' with which he ends is clear: that in some way parents are responsible for autism in their children. Kanner continued to hold this position beyond the 1940s, once suggesting in a 1960 interview in *Time* magazine that all children with autism came from "parents cold and rational who just happened to defrost long enough to produce a child" (Feinstein 2010, 33). Indeed, it was Kanner who coined the phrase 'refrigerator mother,' the most notorious comment attached to the idea of parental causation of autism. Though he would claim later in the 1960s that he had always believed that parents were not to blame for autism in children, and that all of his research pointed to the fact that the condition occurred biologically, his statements nevertheless invited further speculation as to what the link between autism and parenting might be.

What happened next was a combination of large-scale medical practice and individual research similar to that we observed above when noting the emergence of child psychiatry and its importance to the careers of Kanner and Asperger. As the 1950s turned into the 1960s, and more research on autism came to be published, the condition fell within the frame provided by the period's development of psycho-analysis. Even though medical thinking on autism had suggested that the condition was organic, the lack of any confirmed biological marker for diagnosis had invited speculation that it may well be a disorder that resulted from a crisis in the self. Kanner's suggestion that the characters of the parents of children with autism might have a part to play in their children's condition only made such a possibility more attractive, and a wave of psychoanalytic research began to analyze the relationship between autistic children and their parents.

The leader of this research was Bruno Bettelheim, an authoritarian figure who became director of the Sonia Shankman Orthogenic School in Chicago in 1944. Bettelheim, a Viennese Jew, had been interned in both Dachau and Buchenwald concentration camps in 1938 and 1939,

Figure 2.3 Bruno Bettelheim
© Corbis

and was only released as a result of a bizarre gesture by Adolf Hitler, who granted some inmates of the camps amnesty to mark his fiftieth birthday. There is little doubt that Bettelheim came to view autism through the lens of his camp experiences: he claimed to have seen how the horror he witnessed had left individuals withdrawn, isolated, and docile, and in a deeply disturbing generalization taken from such observations, he formed the opinion that the relationship between autistic children and their parents was one that mirrored that which existed between camp inmates and those who guarded and persecuted them. More than anyone else, it was Bettelheim who promoted the idea that the child with autism 'withdraws' from the world, a process that takes place as a result of the 'abnormal' behavior of parents who themselves have a psychological pathology that prevents them from bonding with their child. Once started, this creates a spiral, with the parents ever more distant and the children pushed into further withdrawal as a consequence. The result, Bettelheim stated, was profound autism, and the only cure was to separate the child from the parent.

It is important to state that Bettelheim's ideas, as he worked on them during the 1950s and 1960s, came as no surprise to many medical researchers. Psychoanalysis dominated thinking about personality, and the idea that the self was the core focus for thinking about autism was, as a consequence, seen to be entirely logical. The prominence of pioneers in the links between psychoanalysis and children, such as Melanie Klein and Margaret Mahler, during the period made Bettelheim's position and methods understandable. A man who commanded respect and produced a real sense of awe because of the force of his personality, Bettelheim broke out of the closed circle of medical research to become a figure widely known across the US. He was, in the public mind, *the* specialist on autism, this little known and little understood condition that was thought to be extremely rare. Within the research community, Bettelheim's status as a camp survivor gave him an authority that few felt could be challenged, and although some individuals continued to publish accounts that stressed organic and biological elements to autism (Bernard Rimland's 1964 study, *Autism: The Syndrome and its Implications for a Neural Theory of Behavior* was a landmark text in this regard), they were largely ignored.

Bettelheim's attitude towards parents was savage. He claimed that they prevented ego development in their children because of their own inadequacies, and his continual use of language that stressed parental 'coldness' or 'rigidity' produced despair among those who had children with autism. It is difficult to imagine how challenging it must have been to be the parent of an autistic child in, say, 1960, even though we know there must have been many of them. Living with a child that the public at large would have completely misunderstood, the full weight of medical knowledge would have made it very clear where the blame lay. It is no surprise that many parents in such a position became depressed and, in a cruel irony, often had to undergo psychoanalysis themselves. Of course, if the lives of parents were hard, those with autism themselves received little or no meaningful support or successful therapy, and many were institutionalized for most of their lives.

Bettleheim's identification of the causes of autism was only half the story, however, because his following claim was that, as a result of pin-pointing where the condition came from, he and his team in Chicago were able to produce therapies that had success rates unmatched by any other specialist. In his landmark 1967 book *The Empty Fortress*, a text where the attitude towards childhood autism is given away by the very title, Bettelheim championed his psychoanalytic methods while attacking the ideas of others, and asserted that his treatment methods produced substantial improvement in nearly half of the children in his study. This appeared to be a remarkable vindication of his approach, given that no other treatment came anywhere close to such figures. Bettleheim was, it appeared, the undisputed leader in autism research, the major figure in the field since Kanner, and the only person capable of finding a cure to this mysterious and devastating condition.

The appeal of psychoanalytic approaches to autism lay precisely in this relationship to an idea of cure. Because such approaches dismissed the notion that the condition might originate biologically in the brain and was rather caused by behavior, they offered the potential for productive change. If, the logic ran, autism was caused by psychogenic factors, the 'withdrawal' that the child experienced could be rectified. Appropriate therapy could, it appeared, 'bring back' the child who had been 'lost.' We shall see in Part III the ways in which the search for a cure still occupies a powerful place in our own contemporary discussions of autism, but this fact makes it possible to understand how desperate parents might have submitted themselves and their children to the therapies devised by Bettelheim and his followers. For some, accepting that they were to blame was a price worth paying if it meant that their child could be 'rescued' from autism. That this kind of thinking constituted the condition as a 'problem' goes without saying. For families, autism was frequently asserted to be a 'disaster' or a 'tragedy,' and confirmation that this was the case seemed to come from the highest medical authorities.

Eventually, the seemingly impregnable truth that Bettelheim had created started to crumble. The anti-psychiatry movement of the late 1960s and 1970s began to produce evidence that psychoanalytic treatments were often more harmful than beneficial, and continued work in neurology meant that a clearer understanding of the brain made it easier to suggest that autism might have neurological components. In addition, those who worked with children with autism simply became more and more convinced that Bettelheim was wrong, and doubt began to be expressed about his findings. His claims that nearly half of children responded positively to his treatments was not replicated anywhere else, despite other researchers using similar methods, and the powerful personality that had once conveyed authority was now seen to be the source of deceit. When Bettelheim committed suicide in 1990, a number of students from his Orthogenic School came forward to detail the abuse they had suffered while pupils. Bettelheim had hit those supposedly in his care (beatings appeared to be common) and other stories suggested that several students at the school never had autism, but were rather sent by their parents because of something as commonplace as unruly behavior.

The damage done to those with autism, and to the very idea of how the condition functions in the world, that was perpetuated by Bettelheim and his thinking, cannot be overestimated. Never have the 'facts' of autism proved to be so conclusively wrong. Many lives were ruined, and the ability of medical science to lead in the further understanding of the condition was damaged in ways from which it has still not recovered; many parents in particular are still highly suspicious of medical authority, something we will explore further in Part III in connection to the vaccine scares surrounding autism that marked the period around the millennium. Remarkably, given what is now known about psychoanalytic treatments of the condition, such approaches to autism, and their consequences, still operate in some parts of the world. Feinstein observes that "France still largely follows the psychoanalytic tendency" and that "it remains the principal approach in the francophone region of Switzerland" (Feinstein 2010, 74), while in his book on autism anthropologist Roy Richard Grinker notes that the situation is similar in Argentina, which along with France has "more psychoanalysts per capita than anywhere else in the world" (Grinker 2007, 83) as well as Korea, where cultural pressures on women who choose to work frequently characterize mothers of children with autism as possessing an inability to care (Grinker 2007, 242). There are still parents who are being made to deal with the suggestion that they may be to blame, and still individuals with autism whose lives are hugely misunderstood and who are subject to inappropriate treatment, if any at all.

Not all parents accepted the view of themselves as brutal suppressors of their child's development however, and not all of those with autism were prepared to allow their endless objectification. One consequence of the traumatic history of autism in the 1960s and 1970s, and possibly the only beneficial one, was the rise of the advocacy movements that began to demand better care policies, better education, and greater understanding of the condition. Often parent led in their initial stages, such movements changed the ways in which autism was discussed, and paved the way for the kinds of disability rights campaigns that would follow in later decades. It was an emergence from a long dark tunnel.

10 Organizations and Associations

If we were able to look back to the early 1960s and view a cross-section of all the various issues connected to autism during the period, it would make for sober reflection. The condition was subject to almost wholesale ignorance, among medical specialists as well as the general public. It was often difficult, if not impossible, to get a diagnosis and even if such a fortuitous event occurred there were virtually no services for people with autism and their families. Children would be excluded from school because of perceptions or complaints about their behavior, usually categorized as 'disruptive,' and the prevailing misunderstanding that autism only affected children meant that adults with the condition were invisible, lost to all the various healthcare, social, and educational systems that had no language or structures to meet their needs.

It appeared that the only people who were in any place to develop clear-sighted approaches to autism in the early 1960s were the small number of professionals who resisted the psychoanalytic approach to the condition, and family members who realized that the conceptions that came from such an approach failed to adequately describe those they lived with on a day-to-day basis. In the UK, a group of like-minded parents came together in London to form the Society for Autistic Children (originally called the Society for Psychotic Children) in 1962, while the first autism association in the US was formed in upstate New York in 1963. The National Society for Autistic Children in the US was born out of a number of such small-scale meetings and had its first congress in 1969. Fighting the widespread ignorance of the period, parents had to negotiate with local and state health and educational authorities, many of whom simply referred them to other departments and services, assuming that responsibility lay elsewhere. Slowly, through years of campaigning, these early autism pressure groups helped develop the building blocks of institutional understandings of the condition: first, greater and more sophisticated medical insight; second, social support within the community; and, finally and crucially, special education provision that recognized the specific needs of those with autism. For parents who had been told routinely by professionals that their children were 'uneducable,' this last was a major achievement in particular.

These processes were vital in the development of thinking about autism in a number of ways. One of these was the specificity with which the condition now came to be viewed. At a time when so little was known, it was not easy to assert what was then thought of as the singularity of autism, and to want to differentiate it from the wider category of 'mental handicap.' In the UK, the decision to form the National Society for Autistic Children meant creating distance from Mencap, at that point the largest and most well-known charity dealing with cognitive impairments and mental health. With specialist medical knowledge on autism still in a state of contestation, the decisions of these early pressure groups to demand recognition of the condition as something in its own right was a bold and prescient move. In the UK and US, both these foundational organizations were to go on to become the principle associations supporting those with autism: the British Society for Autistic Children became the National Autistic Society (NAS), while the American National Society for Autistic Children would turn into the Autism Society of America (ASA). The fact that each association dropped the word 'children' from its title displays the increasing understanding that autism was a lifelong condition and that provision needed to be created to meet the requirements of adults with the condition.

In other parts of the world, the move towards a greater understanding of autism has followed similar patterns, but frequently these processes

Figure 2.4 Michael Baron, the first President of the UK's National Autistic Society, in the 1960s
© Baron Family private collection

have taken place far more recently. To cite just one example, in India in the 1980s diagnoses of autism were rare. Most children with the condition were considered 'mentally retarded,' or categorized as 'slow learners' or as having 'behavior problems.' They were often institutionalized and schooled without any specific support; the intervention practiced was identical for all those who fell into these wide classifications, and for those children who did live at home there was no guidance on how a domestic environment might be structured to help with learning and development. A small group of parents came together in Delhi in 1988, sharing their experiences and making contact with psychiatrists, often those with North American training, who could provide a diagnosis. Action for Autism (AFA) was founded as a consequence in 1991, and in 1994 it helped establish a school with just one teacher and two students. In 2005, AFA persuaded the local authorities in Delhi to create a National Centre for Autism, which has been in operation ever since. Despite this, and even with AFA now being the largest autism association in South Asia, knowledge of the condition in India is still very limited, both in the medical profession and the general public, and parents or health workers have to be lucky, or show extraordinary energy and commitment, to find an appropriate diagnosis. Even now, autism is not included in the Indian Persons with Disabilities Act.

The development of these organizations, vital as it has been for the dissemination of knowledge about autism, has not been without controversy. From the 1990s onwards, when advocacy groups began to be set up by those with the condition, there have been concerns about the *idea* of autism with which such associations work, with particular comment that it has been the situations of parents, as opposed to those who are themselves autistic, which have been prioritized. The logo for the NAS, for example, was up until 2003 that of a child who appears to be weeping, hardly the most positive of images (even if the Society itself notes that the image is meant to be a child flapping his hand); while in the US there is considerable hostility towards decisions taken by the ASA by many advocates with autism because of a perceived bias towards parents. It may seem harsh to criticize the associations that have pioneered the ways in which autism is understood, but for some they contain too many characterizations of the condition as a 'tragedy,' or stress questions of absence and loss. The contested relationship between

Figure 2.5 National Autistic Society old logo
© National Autistic Society

major national organizations such as the NAS and ASA and other smaller advocacy and pressure groups is one of the marked features of discussions of autism today. From the outside, this in-fighting appears strange. With so much still to be discovered about the condition it is somewhat perverse for discussions to be characterized in this way by factional hostility. The situation is probably best comprehended in terms of a natural historical process; our knowledge of autism is still limited to the point that all interventions and changes in how the condition is portrayed and presented take place within an unsecure present. It still may well be many years before the parameters of 'thinking autism' are properly established, and the ongoing revisions of the charities and foundations that exist to raise awareness of the condition, however controversial they might be, should be seen within this context.

11 The Rise of Neurodiversity

Demands, Advocacy, and Legislation

The rise of the opinion that autism constitutes a positive difference, and is not a deficit, has been the most noticeable non-medical development in the history of the condition in the last decade. It has been led by those who identify as having autism, and who see it as an integral part of their identity. The wider context for such a change is the development of disability rights more generally, and the demands that the voices of those with disabilities be heard, aligned with the rise of Disability Studies as a socially-inflected academic discipline. These developments take as their base a challenge to the authority of medicalized notions of disability and the assertion of disability within a frame of social difference. From deaf communities to associations for those with physical disabilities, these rights-based movements have changed the ways in which disability is represented and understood.

In the case of autism, the declaration of such rights has involved work undertaken both by individuals and organizations. High profile figures with autism, such as Amanda Baggs, Ari Ne'eman, Jim Sinclair, and Donna Williams have commanded media attention through their arguments that autism constitutes a natural part of neurodiversity. Sinclair and Williams were among the founding members of Autism Network International (ANI), a pioneering advocacy group formed in 1992, and Sinclair's powerful 1993 manifesto 'Don't Mourn for Us' was an early articulation of the rejection of the 'suffering' and 'deficit' model of the condition. Baggs became an immediate celebrity following her posting, in January 2007, of her video 'In My Language' on YouTube (Baggs 2007). When the video, with its powerful presentation of autism as a legitimate mode of being human, went viral, Baggs became the subject of a number of CNN articles discussing the condition (Gajilan 2007; Gupta 2007). For his part, Ne'eman—the founder of the Autistic Self-Advocacy Network (ASAN)—was invited in June 2010 by Barack Obama to become the first autistic member of the National Council on Disability.

Much of this change has been made possible by advances in technology; those with limited language can, for example, be part of forums or movements that have their main presence on the internet. Following the example of the ANI, a number of new associations, such as ASAN or the US-based Aspies For Freedom (AFF), formed in 2004, champion the rights of those with the condition. Other websites, such as neurodiversity.com, gather together vast amounts of information on autism-related issues under the banner of neurological difference. Frequently, these organizations point to instances of ongoing discrimination against individuals with autism, whether at the level of legislation or through specific news stories. They counter the impression that the condition is best characterized by medical progress, rather seeing continued ignorance and prejudice as still being widespread, and that as a consequence the basic rights of individuals still have to be fought for. Such arguments often draw condemnation from others working on autism, who point out that provision for those with the condition has never been better. This back and forth of claim and counter-claim is a marked feature of contemporary issues surrounding autism: especially in the US, where much of the medical research receives funding but also where the rights campaigners are most organized, 'facts' are disputed and opinions stated and challenged. It can be a bewildering environment for many who enter it.

For all of the contestation however, the question of whether autism constitutes a neurological difference possesses an evident clarity. With the increased acceptance that 'classic' autism, as Kanner would have recognized it, is not the only form the condition takes, the knowledge that autism is a spectrum condition means it is easier to see it not *only* as a disability. It is difficult to classify the highly verbal teenager with Asperger's Syndrome, who may well attend mainstream school and be successful academically, as being disabled, even if it is acknowledged that such an individual might have some difficulties in social interaction. And if this scenario is *not* an example of a disability, what exactly is it? The argument that autism, so long conceived of as a 'devastating' disabling condition, might actually illustrate productively the range of human cognitive diversity is a powerful and revealing one. In the ways in which it is increasingly coming to be understood, autism now points to the interface, unfixed and porous, between disability and human variation. It has come to show us that our categories—abled and disabled, abnormal and normal, even sick and healthy—lack the flexibility and detail we require to properly discuss how the brain works. That it is autism, so often portrayed as a condition that highlights what someone does *not* have, that illuminates this 'lack' is, of course, a nice irony.

Partly as a consequence of some of these debates, and partly because of the various campaigns by the associations mentioned above, autism is in the public domain and part of contemporary cultural history as never before. One outcome of this is that it has increasingly achieved a presence in law and legislation. In 1996, the European Parliament produced the Charter of Rights of Persons with Autism, which asserted that those with the condition were entitled to the same rights and privileges as all other Europeans, and called on European Union member states to produce legislation that would enforce this. In the UK, this catalyst, combined with other developments, led to the 2009 Autism Act. The Act is the first piece of national disability-specific legislation, establishing the terms of the provision of care for adults with the condition. Such a development marks a significant increase in profile: autism was not mentioned in any parliamentary legislation in the UK until the 1970 Chronically Sick and Disabled Persons Act, and its inclusion here was within a list of cited conditions that lacked any details specific to the condition itself. In the US, the Combating Autism Act became law in 2006, committing federal funds to aid medical research as well as social and educational services. That autism is a condition seen in terms of 'combat' in the US reflects the widely held opinion that it is something that should be 'fought' or opposed. We will discuss this outlook, and the reaction to it, in Part III, but it is worth acknowledging that alongside those who welcomed the new Act because of its commitment to addressing the condition were others concerned by the characterization the legislation contained, especially the idea that the language suggested autism should be eradicated.

The various institutional histories of autism are ongoing, and they will continue to change as the condition becomes more and more a part of public life. But there is a part of the history of autism, and one that is arguably unique, that has not taken place in the arena of medical research or been defined by pressure groups and parliamentary lobbying. This is the story of autism as a set of *cultural* and *fictional* narratives, one that parallels the other histories discussed here and arguably has had as much effect on forming public opinion as the scientific or advocacy debates. It is a side to autism that has received relatively little analysis and yet exerts considerable power, and it is worth looking at in some detail. What we know about autism may stem from this source more than we fully comprehend.

12 Cultural Representations

Outsider and Insider Accounts

One of the most remarkable aspects of autism is that, for all of the controversies surrounding its medical definitions and the similar debates about treatments and interventions, most people came to know of its existence through a film. Barry Levinson's 1988 feature *Rain Man*, in which Dustin Hoffman played an adult with autism, brought the condition to a level of global public awareness that surpassed anything that had existed prior to this point. It has become a cliché to talk of *Rain Man* in connection with autism, and many who have or work with the condition become weary when it is mentioned, seeing its depiction as dated and increasingly irrelevant. But the importance of the film in historical terms should not be downplayed. It not only created a huge impact in and of itself, but it became the template for many subsequent representations of the condition, depictions that seeped into public consciousness to create ideas about the condition that still exist today. It is hard to think of any other medical condition or disability that has had a similar breakthrough, one where a fictional narrative has seemingly provided central 'facts' about its nature. But, with autism, this is the case.

   Understanding why it was possible for a cultural representation like Levinson's film to achieve such prominence is, in part, another example of 'what we don't know' about autism. In the mid-1980s, at the time of *Rain Man*'s conception, scientific opinion on autism was still sufficiently divided that fiction was able to fill the vacuum created by the lack of consensus. In the absence of any established definition of the condition, a license was given to educated speculation about its manifestations. As it happened, director Levinson and the film's writer, Barry Morrow, went out of their way to consult as many experts on autistic behavior—including a researcher as significant as Bernard Rimland—in order to give the production scientific credibility. For all that they had a story they wished to tell, the filmmakers wanted to ground their portrayal in the available knowledge of the time. That such knowledge was inevitably partial, and that it was necessarily selectively used in the establishment of character and plot, meant that fiction and legitimacy were juxtaposed in the film's representation. The 'accuracy' of the depiction created a version of autism that was taken by many as being factual, even if this was far from the case.

Rain Man centers on the relationship between egotistical debt-ridden Charlie Babbitt (Tom Cruise) and his older brother Raymond (Hoffman) once the former discovers, following his father's death, that the entire family estate has been left to the latter, a sibling that Charlie did not know he had. Feeling that the money is rightfully his, and needing it to pay off his creditors, Charlie takes Raymond from the Ohio institution where he lives, against the wishes of the doctor in charge, and drives him to Los Angeles. On the journey, Charlie's initial prejudices towards Raymond and his autism (he refers to him as a 'retard' on a number of occasions) gives way to understanding and, finally, brotherly love. This culminates in Charlie's attempts, near the end of the film, to argue that Raymond should be allowed to stay in his care. When it becomes clear that this is impossible because of the nature of Raymond's disabilities, Raymond returns to Ohio, with Charlie promising to visit him in the near future.

At heart, the film is a sentimental drama that uses the generic trappings of the road and buddy movie formats to develop the relationship between the brothers. As Charlie learns more about Raymond and his autism, he recognizes the flaws in his own character. This is not a new story: the idea that disability, with its suggestion of both an absence of humanity yet also an excessive humanness created by a physical or mental 'vulnerability,' can provide insight for the non-disabled is a much worn narrative. The 'we-learn-from-them' story is a staple of both film and literature, recognizable from any number of other contexts (its use in race narratives is common for example), and it usually works to objectify the character with any form of difference, here promoting the disabled figure either as a figure worthy of pity or, conversely, of heroic perseverance and achievement (Norden 1994, 313–23). Whatever the dramatic success of the film, in the wake of its release and considerable success (it won four Academy Awards, including those for Best Picture, Best Director, and Best Actor in a Leading Role for Hoffman) it was the representation of autism, rather than the orthodox sentimental narrative of individual growth, that commanded most attention.

Hoffman's portrayal of Raymond created a blueprint for subsequent depictions of autism that lasted until the beginning of the twenty-first century. His performance combined mannered body movements, often awkward and stilted, with a robot-like voice, and both Raymond's movement and speech in the film are noticeably repetitive and limited. Raymond rocks from side to side, avoids eye contact wherever possible, and repeats key phrases to comfort and orient himself during moments of stress. Because of the fact that the idea of an autism spectrum was not fully established by the late 1980s, this physical representation was taken to be evidence of what autism looked like, a template that suggested the signs to be recognized. And this was especially true because of the status of film as a *visual* medium. The majority of the audience who went to see *Rain Man* would never have met anyone with autism, but now here on the screen was a depiction that allowed people to *see* what the condition was like. Understandably, the effect was powerful.

But it was another dimension to Raymond's character that attracted the most attention, and would have profound effects on the public understanding of autism for decades to come. Levinson and Morrow created Raymond as a savant, whose special skills create wonder and awe in all those who meet him. His memory and mathematical abilities allow he and Charlie to win tens of thousands of dollars when gambling in Las Vegas, and this scene is only the highlight among a number of other instances of such apparently inexplicable talent. "He's a genius; he should be working for NASA" Charlie remarks at one point in the film, when Raymond performs seemingly impossible mathematical calculations in a small-town psychiatrist's office. Charlie's awe was matched by that of a curious watching public, which had never seen a portrayal of such abilities in a major commercial feature film. Following the film's release, television programs debated whether such skills were fact or fiction; some even hosted people with autism who were made to answer complicated memory or math questions, in effect performing for the cameras.

Savantism in *Rain Man* created real complexities around autism. First, because of the power of its singular representation, it suggested to many that everyone who had the condition possessed similar skills. In actuality, savant ability, which is produced by specific neurological connections that create 'islands' of concentration in those parts of the brain responsible for calculation and memory, is very rare in those who are autistic. Second, Raymond's savant abilities created autism as a spectacle. In the film, he effectively performs the skills associated with his condition, even if he is only behaving normally in terms of his own self. This sense of performance, heightened by the fact that Hoffman *was* performing of course, connected autism to an idea of behavioral display. The twinning of disability and display has a substantial history, from anatomical exhibitions to Coney Island freak shows, and *Rain Man* created a modern form of what Rosemarie Garland-Thomson has called the "cultural work" of such ideas of display at the end of the twentieth century (Bogdan, 1990; Garland-Thomson 1997, 55–80). The idea that someone with autism might be able to 'do something amazing' contains a desire to *watch* such an event, to see something that appears to be beyond logic or the rational. With the film, autism became fascinating.

It would be unfair to say that the filmmakers should shoulder the responsibility for all these consequences; the desire on the part of the production staff *not* to misrepresent the condition was clear, even if both Levinson and Morrow have admitted that they chose autism for Raymond's character because they believed the condition's emphasis on isolation and a narrow range of interests created powerful metaphors for the kinds of 1980s capitalist excesses they hoped to critique. *Rain Man* also created a market for autism, one based upon the public fascination it produced and, Hollywood being Hollywood, it was not long before other films were made that had the condition as a central focus. From the early 1990s onwards, a number of feature productions (across a range of genres) dramatized autism, often taking their cue from *Rain Man* and including special talents or abilities. This is true of films such as *House of Cards* (1993), *Silent Fall* (1994), *Cube* (1997), and *Mercury Rising* (1998), all different types of film that nevertheless have a character with autism who possesses a special skill. In addition, it is arguable that the success of Levinson's film also created a space for the popular reception of high profile and widely successful features such as *What's Eating Gilbert Grape* (1993) and *Forrest Gump* (1994). During this period, the *Rain Man* stereotype was consolidated and the condition seemingly fixed in the public mind. The suggestiveness of these stories should not be underestimated; they form a kind of 'history' as meaningful as any discussed here.

Since the 1990s, the autism narrative has become more varied. Increased knowledge about Asperger's Syndrome has allowed it to become the subject of feature films, such as *Mozart and the Whale* (2005) and *Adam* (2009), in its own right. Films such as *Snow Cake* (2006), *Ben X* (2007), and *The Black Balloon* (2008) have moved beyond *Rain Man* in portraying 'classic' autism; connections in *Ben X* to social isolation and obsessive gaming, and in *The Black Balloon* to questions of family, have been especially important in developing narratives that speak to greater contemporary understanding of the condition. In addition, the condition in all its forms has become more frequent in literary and television narratives. The global success of Mark Haddon's 2003 novel *The Curious Incident of the Dog in the Night-Time*, a book particularly successful with teenagers, worked in many ways as *Rain Man* had, bringing knowledge of autism to a new generation; and a number of writers with autism—including Tito Rajarshi Mukhopadhyay and Dawn Prince-Hughes—have produced fiction, poetry, and life-writing. In television, it features in a number of types of drama: crime drama often uses a character with the condition as some form of 'silent witness,' while children with autism animate the kinds of family drama in which parental love is tested (and usually celebrated) by the presence of a disabled child. There are more documentaries made about the condition now, and autism has even made it to reality television; in the UK, 2010 saw 'Autistic Superstars,' focusing on musical performance, and 'Autistic Driving School,' both programs made by major corporations. The mere existence of a multi-part series devoted to portraying how those with autism learn to drive signals that we have come a long way from the 'wonder' of the late 1980s.

In part the various cultural narratives of autism have simply run parallel to the condition's increasing presence in society as a whole. As we have played catch up with the facts of autism and sought greater definition and clarity as to its manifestations, we have also produced more stories about it. But the relationship between narratives about the condition and the increasing general knowledge around it is more complex than this: we think more about autism now because it seems to fit with our appreciation of our own time as one dominated by technology, for example, and the easy associations between autism and computing (the 'hard wiring of the brain' etc.) create clear metaphors that seem apt when we consider how the condition reflects our contemporary moment. And this idea of the brain being 'wired' in certain ways works to remind us that we are more interested in neurology now than we have ever been; the ways in which neurology has come to replace psychology as a mechanism for understanding human behavior has been a noticeable feature of the last decade, and not simply at the level of scientific research. Here again autism seems the zeitgeist condition, a way of being in the world which makes these associations seem that bit clearer. At the same time, however, part of the continued fascination with autism is still precisely that it suggests things that are *beyond* technology, science, or rational thought. The increased focus on the condition has not reduced its status as an enigma or mystery; it still talks to what we don't know in ways that are powerful, and arguably this too fulfills a need. We like stories that take us beyond our comprehension, and as long as the causes of autism remain unclear then this aspect of portraying the condition will, in all probability, continue.

13 Conclusion

History in the Making

All medical histories are unfinished in the sense that ongoing research revises what we know about the body and mind, but it is fair to say that this is more the case with autism than with other conditions. As this section has shown, much of the history of the condition has been recent, and we should be aware when we talk about autism that we are very much *in* the formative historical stages; it is very likely, for example, that the singular category of 'autism' will not be able to hold all the different variants of the condition that will be come to be understood, and old categories may well be superseded by new. There is speculation that Asperger's Syndrome might be removed from *DSM-V* because of new ideas surrounding the proper description of the condition. All the research, scholarship, arguments, and opinions being produced now may well look very strange when viewed from the perspective of hundreds of years in the future. The history of autism at that point may see our thoughts and interventions as the actions of those stumbling in the dark.

At the same time, the history of a period such as that dominated by Bruno Bettelheim reminds us that the need to clarify and seek knowledge is a process that the present demands. Whatever the arguments that have taken place in the past, there have been significant developments through the historical changes of the last 50 years. For all that the medical research produced in the second half of the twentieth century remains pivotal to our ability to discuss autism today, possibly the central fact that has emerged from a consideration of that history is that people with autism are no longer thought to be useless. The 'natural' assumption that those with the condition would never develop, and could offer nothing to society, was common even 30 years ago. But if we look at the ways in which all the various historical factors interact, we see that the shapes that emerge point to the growing legitimacy of the life lived with autism. It is true that ignorance and misunderstanding still surround the condition, and that misrepresentations are common, sometimes with painful consequences, but our own historical moment *values* autism as never before. It is no longer the default position to believe that all those with the condition lead lives that are tragic, and the difficult history that has led us to this point therefore has to be seen in terms of achievement, for all that the situation is far from perfect. If, in the contemporary period, history is seen less as the parade of grand narratives and more the product of small or everyday activities, then the simple fact that we can talk of day-to-day autism, even 'ordinary' autism, free from the sense that it is an abstract force, somehow 'out there' and beyond us, is a real milestone.

Despite this, however, that supposed writer of a future history of autism may well look back at the early decades of the twenty-first century and choose to characterize them as a period of controversy, because differences of opinion and conflict are still common. There are those who would disagree, perhaps passionately, with the sentiments

I have just expressed in the last paragraph, seeing them as optimistic and naive, or feeling that they miss the point altogether. For some, autism is a difficult and horrendous condition that we would all be better off without; those who feel this would like the history of autism to belong firmly to the past with no kind of future. It is entirely appropriate that the final third of this book is devoted to the controversies that surround the condition, because there are so many and they produce such strong feelings. Part of understanding autism today lies in trying to plot a path through the controversial present, something that is by no means straightforward.

PART III
MAJOR CONTROVERSIES

14 A Lack of Consensus

A number of the major controversies surrounding autism have already been discussed in Parts I and II of this book. The complexities surrounding diagnosis and the differences of opinion about treatment, for example, are frequently very controversial, and arguably there has been no greater controversy than the damage done to those with autism, and their families, during the period when psychoanalytic approaches to the condition dominated medical thinking. But it is the contemporary controversies and the arguments of the here and now that I want to focus on in the final third of this study. Roy Richard Grinker has termed the discussion of autism at the start of the twenty-first century as a "perfect storm" (Grinker 2007, 172) of competitive claims to knowledge. Such a storm has arisen because of a number of interrelated factors, all a product of the increased attention the condition has received in the last decade. These include the widening of the diagnostic criteria for autism and greater referral to doctors, but also the juxtaposition of such advances in medical knowledge with the opinions of those non-specialists who, often because of a perception of autism's history, cannot bring themselves to trust that knowledge. They also include the substantial increase in media coverage of the condition, in which any new autism development has frequently received widespread comment and opinion, whatever its veracity. To repeat something that has been a dominant theme of this book, these controversies stem frequently from what we don't know about autism; the space that the absence of consensus has created has made it easy for argument and counter-argument to flourish.

The first big issue in contemporary autism controversies surrounds causation; the fact that still eludes medical research. The battle of opinions over what causes autism has taken significant new turns since the rejection of the psychodynamic 'bad parenting' model, moving now to include questions of environment, toxins, and even conspiracy theories about government collusion with the pharmaceutical industry. The second highly controversial topic is that of whether autism can be cured, or whether this is even an appropriate question to ask given what we now know about the condition. As we shall see, the debate over any potential cure creates passion and hostility on all sides in a manner that few other topics connected with autism can rival. The arguments over cause and cure are especially important because their terms often guide the fundraising activities of the major foundations that pay for research into autism. Winning the debate over what is deemed to be important in relation to autism, and why, may well unlock the money that will pay for the medical studies that determine future directions of thinking about the condition.

In this section, I will look at these two broad areas and the numerous issues that come under their respective headings. I will then move out from this to consider how they affect those who live with autism and what conclusions we can draw about the relationship between the condition and humanity. Again, it is important to reinforce the fact that all conversations about autism that confine themselves to the abstract, to only the *idea* of what might cause the condition for example, run the risk of ignoring the very people who are the reason for the discussion in the first place. Far too often, the heat and light created by autism controversies are disassociated from the realities of those who have the condition, and a lot of energy is wasted that could more profitably be used in thinking about actual autistic lives. The classic disability slogan, 'Nothing About Us Without Us,' is as true of autism as of any other condition of disability; what writer with autism Richard Attfield has called becoming "'talked about' instead of 'included'" is still more common than not (Biklen 2005, 240). There is a real need to understand why people argue as they do about autism, but there is an equal need to make sure that those arguments are made meaningful through a connection to those they most centrally concern.

15 Causing Autism

If there is consensus that autism is now understood to be a neurobiological condition, with associated genetic influences, there is still significant debate about *why* the brain in those with the condition might develop as it does. Is this something that is pre-determined in the womb, either as a question of inheritance or because of some event *in utero*? Or might it be connected to the ways that the brain grows and changes after birth, a process that might be organic or one that could be influenced by external factors? There are arguments that seem to supply evidence for a range of possibilities: genetic research suggests the importance of inheritance, while our understanding of the ways in which the brain develops during the first years of life points to the possibility that it might be during this period that the structures of the brain responsible for autism take their final form; and, in support of potential external causes, one of the most-repeated observations about the development of autism in the very young is that the onset of the condition appears to happen suddenly around the age of two. Up to that point, some parents observe, their child displays no signs of autism and appears to be developing in line with other children. In these cases, autism appears to arrive unheralded, and it seems only natural to assume that there is some cause for the change, something that happens. It should be stressed that such opinions are usually anecdotal, and no research has given any indication of the commonality of this kind of onset of the condition, but it is a point of view made with some regularity by a number of parent groups.

Working out which of the above fits where, or even which is correct, in understanding the causes of autism has occupied many minds in the last decade. This has appeared as a particularly pressing debate because of the claims that we have witnessed an autism 'epidemic' during this period. The argument that there has been an epidemic is based on the fact that there are more diagnoses of autism now than there have ever been in history, and that this comes at a time when more is known about the condition than ever before, a fact that should lead to more accuracy in the diagnostic process. Much is made of the fact that current thinking has established that autism affects around 1 in every 110 people, whereas in the 1970s it was closer to 1 in 2,000. How else can this be described but as an epidemic? As Grinker has observed, the word itself evokes significant reactions:

> "Epidemic" is a powerful concept. It implies danger and incites fear, calling up associations with plagues that can sweep through the streets, something contagious in the air that you breathe or in the food you eat, threatening the ones you love. With autism, the label of "epidemic" sounds both frightening and tragic.
>
> (Grinker 2007, 5)

The idea of contagion is indeed a frightening one. Of course it is impossible to 'catch' autism from another person, but what if it can be 'caught' in some other way, from another entity, one that surrounds us or can enter our bodies in some fashion? 'Epidemic' seems to suggest that such an event might indeed be possible; indeed it appears to be proof that it is already taking place.

We shall return to the issue of increased diagnosis, but for now we might consider what it was that might have suggested to some that this kind of contagion has been happening, given the fact that scientific research has, for a number of years, showed this not to be the case (Gernsbacher, Dawson, and Goldsmith 2005; S.R. Kaufman 2010). Broadly, such thinking falls into two camps: first, that there is some environmental aspect that is proving to be toxic for those who might be in some way susceptible (such as those with a genetic predisposition) to developing autism; and second that it is caused by vaccination, the deliberate introduction into the body of elements that affect the structure of the brain in a manner that allows the condition to develop. One example of the environmental argument was put forward in 2006, when Michael Waldman and fellow scholars at Cornell University suggested in a 66-page working report that a growth in autism among children was due to an increase in the provision of cable television combined with precipitation levels that forced children inside to watch more television than they might if the weather was less wet. Waldman and his co-authors looked at data from a number of counties in three US states—California, Oregon, and Washington—and found that the rise in the occurrence of autism in children matched the spread of available cable television in rainy locations. In 2008, Waldman and his associates published some of the findings—those connected to precipitation, the television link having been dropped—in the journal *Archives of Pediatrics and Adolescent Medicine.*

The original 2006 report generated much discussion. 'Does Watching TV Cause Autism?' asked Claudia Wallis in an article so titled which was published in the October 2006 edition of *Time* magazine. Noting that searching for the causes of the rise in rates of autism was "one of the most anguishing mysteries of modern medicine," Wallis picked up on the claim in Waldman's study that nearly 40 percent of autism diagnoses in the three states in the study were the result of television watching due to precipitation. In her article, Wallis was clearly skeptical about the findings, though interestingly one of the ways that she suggested its limitations was to cite *other* possible environmental factors, such as indoor air quality, or levels of mold and mildew produced by heavy rain. Wallis signed off with the observation that "There are probably many routes to the disorder, involving diverse combinations of genes and noxious environmental influences. Could Teletubbies be one of them?" (Wallis 2006). There was no doubt that this was a good story.

At the heart of the environment/contagion argument is a worry that the way we lead our modern lives might be poisoning our children. It is no coincidence that it is television-watching that is highlighted in the Waldman report, since its powerful status as an example of potentially troubling technology is frequently cited in debates surrounding child development. We all know children watch too much television, the logic appears to run, and that this probably isn't good for them; what if, in fact, it is so bad for them it causes autism? Here we are back with the idea of autism and metaphor discussed in Part I, with the condition becoming attached to a contemporary fear (that society is failing its children) because of its status as some kind of enigmatic, mysterious, unknowable—and yet malign—force. In their defence, Waldman and his co-authors would probably point to the fact that their study was based on statistical evidence, but that in turn only again serves to remind us of the fact that what we don't know about autism allows for all kinds of conclusions, including statistical ones, to be drawn from a contemplation of its seemingly elusive quality.

Even if it is proved that there is some kind of interaction between a predisposition to autism (whether that be genetic or some other physical form) and an environmental aspect that serves to trigger the condition, it is safe to say that the idea that watching television in wet weather causes autism is one example where we can dismiss the notion that an academic study is producing any kind of 'fact' worth consideration. It is far more likely that what is at work here belongs to the realm of culture at least as much as that of science. Inherent in a number of the environmental theories of autism causation (others include overhead power lines and exposure, of the child or pregnant mother, to pesticides and other chemicals) is a worry that we live in a toxic age, and that this must somehow seep into our bodies in ways we have yet to understand. This also, of course, establishes autism as exactly the kind of fearful contagion suggested by Grinker; a silent predator that spreads among an innocent population of children. And, in turn, if autism is constituted as some kind of poison, it becomes very difficult to make the argument that it is a form of human variation; we do not react well to thinking of difference in terms of some kind of noxious disease.

The idea of poisoning is also central to the very high profile argument that autism is caused by vaccination. Again, the question here is one of toxins, specifically the use of heavy metals, such as mercury, as preservatives in vaccines. One such preservative is Thimerosal (known outside the US as Thiomersal), which is nearly half mercury in its make-up by weight. In 1999, the American Food and Drug Administration (FDA) published a report noting that children who received multiple vaccinations that contained Thimerosal were being exposed to levels of mercury that were significantly above federal guidelines. The outcry this caused was understandable: in excessive amounts, mercury is a known neurotoxin, and the administration of too much of it, especially to children, is certainly a danger. The FDA report could only cause concern, especially as it appeared on the back of an even more significant publication which, although it did not cause much controversy at first, came to dominate the arguments surrounding autism and vaccination.

In 1998, the gastroenterologist Andrew Wakefield, working at the Royal Free Hospital in London, was the lead author of a study investigating development disorders, including autism, in a number of children. The study, published in the leading British medical journal the *Lancet*, focused on bowel symptoms and findings produced by biopsies and endoscopies, among others (Wakefield et al. 1998). According to the parents of some of the children involved, the onset of the symptoms had taken place very close to the time they were given the combined Measles, Mumps and Rubella (MMR) vaccine. The paper itself did not suggest that the MMR vaccine was a trigger for autism, though it did indicate that there was a real connection between gastrointestinal illness and autism, and that the measles virus in the vaccine caused infection in the intestine that allowed harmful proteins to enter into the bloodstream and work their way into the brain. It also recommended that there should be further research undertaken on whether the vaccine was in any way connected to autism, and in the press conference publicizing the research, Wakefield declared a lack of confidence in the combined vaccine, advocating that it would be best if the three vaccines were delivered separately.

Initially, and despite some front page headlines the day after the press conference, reporting on the *Lancet* paper was relatively low key, but in the two years that followed, and especially as Wakefield made more claims for the lack of safety of immunization, the controversy grew. That this coincided with the FDA report on Thimerosal only increased attention, even given the fact that the preservative was not actually used, and never had been, in the MMR vaccination. In the US, an Institute of Medicine (IOM) committee was established in 2001 to review the safety issues surrounding immunization, looking at both Thimerosal and MMR. Late in that year it published an interim report that said there was no evidence to suggest any causal link between Thimerosal and the development of autism, though it also suggested that it was sensible to remove the preservative from vaccines given

Figure 3.1 The scare surrounding possible links between immunization and autism has been the subject of intense media speculation

© Barbara Bellingham/Wellcome Images

to babies, children, and pregnant women. It also observed that the hypothesis that developmental conditions could be caused by vaccines that contained Thimerosal was one that had biological plausibility, and that "the committee notes that its conclusion does not exclude the possibility that MMR vaccine could contribute to autism spectrum disorder in a small number of children" (Offit 2008, 209).

In 2004, the IOM committee published a final report, which included results taken from epidemiological surveys in a number of nations, concluding that there was no link between either the MMR vaccine, or those containing Thimerosal, and autism, and that vaccines were proven to be safe in any number of studies. But by then it was too late to stop the controversy. The very idea that toxins were present in vaccines, combined with the continuing publicity surrounding Wakefield's research, and the seemingly less-than-conclusive statements by official bodies such as the IOM in its early investigations of possible links to autism, created a media firestorm. Before long, other researchers began to publish studies noting associations between vaccine toxins and autism, even suggesting that the condition itself was a new form of mercury poisoning. That this research was not appearing in peer-reviewed journals, and that many of those producing it were not vaccine experts, toxicologists, or epidemiologists, seemed of little concern, especially to a media that sensed a huge public story. Influential feature articles in widely read magazines, such as *Time* and *Rolling Stone*, and front page reports in many newspapers not only reported on the link between immunization and autism, but also suggested possible cover ups by health institutions because of the threat to their relationships with pharmaceutical companies. In 2005, journalist David Kirby published *Evidence of Harm*, a 460-page book that had as its subtitle 'Mercury in Vaccines and the Autism Epidemic: A Medical Controversy.' In great detail, Kirby both dissected the arguments of the previous few years and dramatized conversations and events, celebrating parents and damning the authorities for failing to prevent children falling into what he termed the "shuttered hell of autism" (Kirby 2005, 3). The anti-vaccine movement had a number of vocal and very influential champions.

Questions went right to the top of government. Starting in April 2000, House of Representatives member Dan Burton, who has a grandson with autism, convened a number of congressional hearings on the topic, convinced that vaccines were a problem and accusing the federal administration of a failure of responsibility. In the hearings, Burton argued that there was no doubt that there was an autism epidemic, and engaged in vociferous arguments with senior political opponents and representatives from the Centers for Disease Control and Prevention. And, in what was arguably the most worrying development of all, public concerns over the vaccine led to a fall in immunization rates. In the UK especially, where reporting of Wakefield's work was most prominent, confidence in the MMR vaccine fell to 41 percent, with some parents too worried to have their children vaccinated. Overall, the take-up rate for the vaccination fell from over 90 percent before the *Lancet* article, to below 80 percent in the years following, not increasing again until 2005.

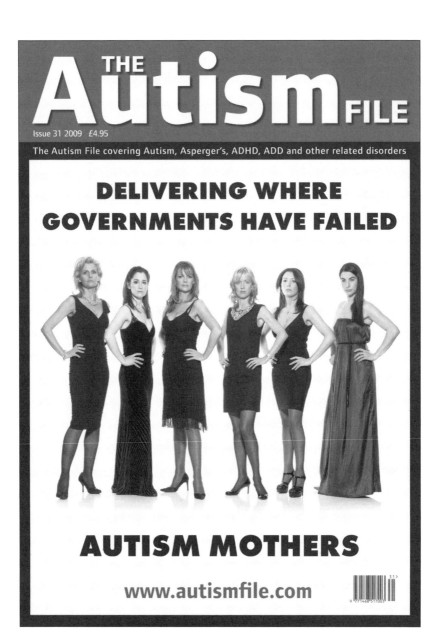

Figure 3.2 Cover of *The Autism File* magazine in 2009, stressing the role of parent power in the face of perceived government ignorance

© *The Autism File*

Figure 3.3 Cover of *The Autism File* magazine in 2010, emphasizing the place of parent power
© *The Autism File*

In the middle of such outcry, autism was characterized firmly as a disaster. It was a condition to be argued about more than understood, thrown this way and that between differing opinion groups and delivered to a dazed public as a kind of nightmare. Stories reproduced in the national press told of parents watching as their child regressed into autism before their very eyes in the days after vaccination, becoming 'lost' in the grip of some horrific visitation. The very idea of 'regressive autism,' for some a subset of the wider condition, came to dominate much media reporting. Autism 'took children away,' and the idea that this was due to some failure of medical authority made the situation unbearable. The general suspicion that scientific and medical research was too distant from the public, and that this was true of government associations as well, became full blown. Wakefield was hailed as the people's champion, a heroic figure standing up to both big business and big government: "Everything I know about autism," he told a Canadian interviewer in 2000, "I know from listening to parents" (Murray 2008, 189). He was even the subject of a television drama, entitled *Hear the Silence*, which screened in the UK in December 2003 and which characterized him in just such laudable terms, while making it clear that drug companies had a vested interest in suppressing the truth. Those parents who did object to the anti-vaccine arguments, not wanting to see their children defined as hosts of toxins and poisons, found themselves in a minority and were often subject to abuse and censure. The various national health associations around the world, unable to prevent the furore that, in part, their own lack of ability to respond had created, appeared to be powerless and helpless.

From 2004, however, things began to change. Following the publication of Wakefield's paper, study after study looking at the same research questions found no link between vaccination and the development of autism. In addition, from the start of the year onwards newspaper reports began to investigate a possible conflict of interest surrounding his research, after it emerged that, before the *Lancet* article was published, Wakefield had accepted money on behalf of a law firm representing anti-vaccine campaigners and that a number of the parents who had identified the MMR vaccine as the cause of their children's autism were also litigants in the action. Unaware that this had been the case when pursuing their original research, in March 2004 10 of

Wakefield's *Lancet* co-authors retracted any possible interpretation that the vaccine might be linked to the condition. In 2007, the UK's General Medical Council, the body responsible for the supervision of doctors and the implementation of medical ethics, began an investigation into Wakefield's conduct, analyzing both the possible conflict of interest and the fact that he and his research team had failed to obtain the necessary permissions when working with the children in his study. In February 2010, the *Lancet* retracted the 1998 paper, removing it completely from the published record, and in May 2010, having been found guilty of serious professional misconduct, Wakefield was struck off the medical register, barring him from practicing medicine in Britain.

Also in 2010, and following hearings that had started in 2007, the US Court of Federal Claims ruled that Thimerosal does not cause autism, backing up a similar ruling made in 2009. Over 5,300 claims that had been filed by the parents of children with autism, arguing that vaccines were responsible for their child's condition, were brought before a special 'Vaccine Court,' part of the federal Vaccine Injury Compensation Program that exists to provide compensation if it is proved that children are harmed by vaccination. Three individual test cases, in effect the circumstances of three autistic children, were heard before the court in great detail to determine the wider claim. In all three cases, the court ruled that vaccines were not responsible for the development of autism in the children concerned. The latest ruling is subject to appeal, but it seems to be clear that the tide has turned against the anti-vaccine movement.

There is no evidence to suggest autism is caused by immunization. A number of epidemiological studies from 2003 onwards, using ever more complex methodologies, have shown that rates of the condition increased even after Thimerosal was removed from vaccines, or even if (as has been the case in Japan) the three elements of the MMR were given to children separately. The controversy that suggested that inoculation might be the cause has been, however, the most visible discussion of the condition in the last decade. The 'perfect storm' identified by Grinker was, at its height, arguably almost as damaging as Bruno Bettelheim's thesis surrounding causation in the 1960s. Blame for this should not simply be laid at the door of certain individuals or groups who pursued specific ideas or theories, although the culture of personal injury litigation, in the US in particular, has created an industry in which claims against vaccine safety have become a business. The failure of medical authorities to reassure the public itself betrayed confusion about the condition, and the culpability of the media in chasing stories displayed how there is still a clear desire to sensationalize autism in terms of 'mystery.' The sharp rise in the number of diagnoses seen in the last 10 years is almost certainly due to a number of overlapping issues: a broadening of the criteria in assessing the condition (to include, for example, more cases of Asperger's Syndrome); increased knowledge, on the part of both the public and medical practitioners, which has resulted in more referrals; the fact that the old statistics may well have been inaccurate because of limits in how autism was understood; greater precision in research, which has led to improvements in epidemiological methods and more standardization in the sizes of sample groups and measurements used; and a simple tendency, now that autism is more well known, for the diagnosis to be given in borderline cases where, in previous years, another label may have been applied. For all the passion surrounding the topic, there is no epidemic, there is simply change.

Where this leaves the debates about the causes of autism is in a quieter, if still unsure, space. As we saw in Part I, there is still no certainty about causation, or indeed about the exact boundaries research should follow, and this may well remain the case for some considerable time. In such an absence of knowledge, and the subsequent legitimate concerns about the way the condition is characterized and discussed, there are still those who will believe in the various toxins arguments, and indeed Wakefield still has his supporters. People are still convinced by what they sense is true, despite the clear medical evidence to the contrary; as Paul Offit reports in *Autism's False Prophets*, one clinician giving evidence at the US Congressional hearings on the subject stated her certainty that autism was caused by vaccines "regardless of what the research tells us" (Offit 2008, 207). More than anything else, the question of what causes autism is symptomatic of our need to know, to deal with the issues of interpretation with which we started this book. In spite of this, it is worth acknowledging that it is highly likely that knowing the cause of the condition would not affect the lives of many who are autistic, nor those of their families. Having autism, or living with it, will not be rectified by being able to push some button that might be available should a cause be found. Undoubtedly, if it is ever possible, locating a cause will be vital in addressing issues surrounding early intervention in the lives of some who are autistic, but there will be others for whom it will make no difference at all; a life with autism will still be exactly that. *Knowing* what causes autism will, however, be hugely important, not just because of the ways in which it makes further research possible, but because it will fill in a blank and satisfy a desire for an idea of completion. In addition, it might reduce the kinds of misadventures that have marked the last 15 years.

Such misadventures will go down in the history of autism as part of a major controversy. But the arguments about causation, however heated they may have been, appear to be in a minor key when placed next to those surrounding the question of whether autism is a condition that should be cured. There is continuity between the two questions of course: some of the parents involved in the vaccination debates were animated by the belief that establishing a cause would make a potential cure available, and some of the ideas about curing came from the causation debate; but the majority of families involved appeared to have wished mainly for ways to care for their children as effectively as possible. There are those, however, who believe that it is viable, and indeed desirable, to counter the 'regression' into autism, to 'rescue' individuals from their lives with the condition or to look for early indications that might then be corrected. These beliefs, when set against those of others who see them as a threat to their very existence, make for a highly combustible mix, and another huge controversy that goes to the very heart of what autism is.

16 Autism and the Idea of the Cure

There is a point that should be made right at the start of our discussion of this topic, one similar to that made in the conclusion to Part I. All serious research into autism acknowledges that it is a lifelong condition and that it is built into the fabric of the person who has it. It is, as we noted earlier, not an illness. As such, it cannot be cured. Why, then, does anyone think that the opposite might be true? What is it that somehow does not communicate itself about this aspect of the condition? Here, what is meant by the word 'cure' when used in relation to autism is especially instructive. Some would disagree with my first four sentences above, asserting that the research is wrong and indeed that autism *can* be cured, in the sense of being made to go away, and in this context it is also discussed in terms of words like 'recovery' and 'healing.' Others talk of cure to mean a process of making things better, of eliminating the most disabling aspects of the condition, in the way that the word might be applied to a process of treatment. For another group, the word 'cure' is a threat, a barely disguised attempt to define difference as something inherently negative and unwanted. Some want a cure with considerable passion and others oppose its place in any debate with equal intensity. These, we might feel, are all interesting positions given our starting point here: that autism cannot be cured.

For all that the question of curing autism appears to be a scientific debate, it is wise to see it, as with so much about the condition, in terms of metaphor. Autism often appears as something which children in particular 'descend into,' or become 'lost in.' That this description is frequently combined with an idea of the condition being 'hellish' only reinforces the notion that, rather than being discussed in terms of scientific rationalism, some depictions of autism seem more aligned with the 'Purgatorio,' if not the 'Inferno,' sections of Dante's *Divine Comedy*. As we shall see, both the metaphorical and the religious aspects of such a symbolic link do indeed play a significant part in the debate surrounding curing. The language of curing autism is about reclamation, saving, and rescue, processes often seen in terms of acts of faith.

As an example, in 2005 Californian financier J.B. Handley, who has a son with autism, founded an organization called Generation Rescue, a movement devoted to publicizing the 'truth' that children with the condition had been poisoned by mercury. Generation Rescue used Handley's wealth and the support of others to take out full-page adverts in many US newspapers, including the *New York Times*, to outline its position. It established a network of 'Rescue Angels,' parents of children with autism who provided a community of helpers to others in similar situations. Armed with the idea of angelic rescue, Generation Rescue made provocative and highly public interventions in the vaccine debates, asserting that autism is a result of the introduction of toxins into children and that it can be reversed. Indeed, "Autism is Reversible" is one of the banner headlines on the current Generation Rescue website, along with advice on how to "recover your child from autism." The organization is now fronted by the celebrity Jenny McCarthy, like Handley also the parent of a son with the condition, and a guest on a number of major television network talk shows in the last three years. McCarthy's 2007 book, *Louder Than Words*, detailed her journey to 'heal' her son Evan, whose autism was suggested to her, McCarthy asserts, in a number of "hints" from God (Generation Rescue 2010).

The explicit religious language that surrounds a project such as that of Generation Rescue sets spirituality against medical research, although it is interesting that the organization does seek some degree of scientific legitimacy through an association with those studies that agree with its position on mercury and vaccines. The symbolism of autism being a 'descent into hell' finds its corollary in the idea of a divinely-inspired rescue, a cure that is miraculous because of the manner of return it enables. These kinds of discourse, and metaphors, suffuse the cure movement, even down to the detail of the methods by which autism can be removed from the child who has it. Generation Rescue and a number of other anti-vaccine groups advocate the use of chelation therapy, a chemical process by which toxic mercury is drawn out of the body through the application of a synthetic amino acid that binds with the mercury and eliminates the heavy metal, and one that has proven medical effects in dealing with acute toxic metal poisoning. Handley claimed to see a dramatic improvement in his own son following the daily application of a chelation chemical which was rubbed into his son's legs and forearms, and other parents have noted similar results. The laying-on of hands to expel autism in this way has an overt religious dimension, one matched by the 'recovery' that takes place as a consequence. If this is not an explicit act of exorcism (and, as we saw in Part I, such activities have been performed on autistic children) it comes very close to being so.

Chelation therapy is a favorite method of treatment for anti-vaccine supporters. It is very expensive and scientific testing has produced no evidence that it has any effect whatsoever in treating autism (Weber and Newmark 2007). But such concerns are not important when it is a question of belief or proclamation of faith that is required. It is not the only 'miraculous' procedure that has been claimed to cure autism. In 1998 and 1999, the use of secretin, a hormone that controls secretions in the body, was similarly championed as a breakthrough in treating the condition. A number of children injected with secretin were seen to display improvements in speech and eye contact almost immediately after its introduction, creating a huge demand (and a significant price tag) for the substance. Medical tests in the years that followed determined that secretin actually produced no more difference in the development of children with autism than similar forms of treatment using a saline solution, but the *idea* of the miracle cure was a powerful phenomenon that, for many, transcended the slow and dry process of proof derived through medical research.

Curing autism, it seems, invites miracles. One of the most well-known, longstanding, and public processes of treating the condition is the Son-Rise program, established by Barry and Samahria Kaufman, and run out of the Autism Treatment Center of America in Massachusetts. Son-Rise, for all that its origins lie in the treatment the Kaufmans developed for their own son Raun, makes the notion of resurrection clear through its very title. The attention the Kaufmans have received has made their program mainstream, and the nature of its claims to transformation is clear: they have published books, *To Love Is To Be Happy With: The Miracle of One Autistic Child* (1976), *A Miracle To Believe In* (1981), and *Son-Rise: The Miracle Continues* (1994), been the subject of a 1979 television film—*Son-Rise: A Miracle of Love*—and toured extensively promoting their approach to autism therapy, based on motivating parents and interaction with children. The sheer preponderance of miracles in the Son-Rise story arguably threatens to make them commonplace rather than exceptional, but the message is clear: recovery and cure from autism is possible if enough belief exists.

Raun Kaufman's recovery allowed him, in his own words, "to emerge from the shell of my autism without a trace of my former condition" (Kaufman 1994, xiii). It is this last phrase—"without a trace of my former condition"—that is so inviting to those who seek to cure autism.

The purging of the body to remove the condition, however it might be achieved, is the ultimate goal. That this creates an idea of autism as either a toxin or some form of malevolent presence goes without saying, and the language of combat that accompanies such characterization enhances this notion of the battle required to remove the condition. 1995 saw not only the formation of the highly influential foundation Cure Autism Now (CAN), but also that of Defeat Autism Now! (DAN!—the exclamation mark is an official part of the title, suggesting a sense of urgency), based at the Autism Research Institute in San Diego. That curing and defeating might go hand in hand in this manner only gives the conflict metaphor greater clarity, and we have seen already how such language made its way into the 2006 Combating Autism Act. In 2007, CAN merged with Autism Speaks, currently the largest autism global foundation, and an organization that—as its website claims—has raised more than $89 million to fund autism research since 1997 (Autism Speaks 2010). For its part, Defeat Autism Now! continues to operate regular research conferences and workshops.

If defeating autism carries overtones of religious fervor and 'the good fight,' then healing the condition suggests a different kind of spiritual approach. The enigmatic nature of autism has always acted as an invitation for holistic theories about its causes and manifestations. For some, its status as a mystery means that, in seeking to understand it, we need to look beyond the boundaries of rational, scientific, or institutional thought. As such, accounts of the condition that link it to New Age spiritualities or the recovery of lost knowledge systems have considerable appeal. Free from obsessions with chemical treatments and medical studies, such treatment techniques explore autism within links to pre-modern beliefs, where intuitive connections create insights into the condition. In the 1980s, for example, the theory that swimming with dolphins could provide a breakthrough in treating autistic behaviors had substantial support, for all that the particulars of such a connection could not be understood. If modern research into genetics or neurobiology might suggest that these kinds of ideas might have lost their appeal, in fact the opposite is true. A book such as Rupert Isaacson's *The Horse Boy: The True Story of a Father's Miraculous Journey to Heal His Son*, which was published in 2009 to considerable acclaim and moved quickly onto both the *New York Times* and the

Sunday Times bestseller lists in the US and UK, before being made into a documentary film that had official selected screenings at a number of major independent film festivals, is only the latest example of a narrative in which spiritual 'healing' counters the presence of an invidious and crippling autism.

But one straightforward fact about autism is forgotten in these various accounts of progress. The condition is one of *developmental delay*. Autism is not some kind of static state into which an individual regresses, never to change. Children with autism might not develop speech when two years old, but a number will do so before they are ten; they may avoid all eye contact when they are three, but will happily hold the gaze of a parent, and clearly respond to emotions, when they are twelve. More than anything else, stories of curing and healing autism are indicative of a belief that change is possible and that, when it comes, it is somehow 'miraculous.' The idea that the change being witnessed may well just be normal, part of a process of development that may not be that of children who are not autistic, but is development nonetheless, appears to be somehow too ordinary to warrant comment, even if it is something that takes place all the time. Like all children, children with autism grow up. That some forget this is indicative of the extent to which the idea of the condition being 'tragic' is still ingrained in contemporary culture.

Those who are autistic themselves often view the curing or healing debates with a mixture of hostility and resigned weariness. The hostility is reserved for the advocates of aggressive or invasive chemical treatments and for those who seek to transform individuals with autism, without any thought for their consent, into something else. The Aspies For Freedom website makes opposition to any idea of a cure explicit in its mission statement, noting that "dangerous non-medically approved therapies based on discredited theories or religious belief" and "therapies that would be called 'torture' if they were used on non-autistic children" are still all too prevalent. "To 'cure' someone of autism," the mission statement continues, "would be to take away the person they are, and replace them with someone else" (Aspies For Freedom 2010). Equally, the Autistic Self Advocacy Network (ASAN) cites the need to "change public perceptions of autism and to dispel old myths and stereotypes that have led to discrimination and abuse" in outlining its commitment to a greater social understanding of the condition (ASAN 2010). The weariness comes from having to experience endless narratives in which autism, seen as a tragedy, is the subject of 'heroic' overcoming. "We're the ones who live the consequences of what anyone says (or publishes) about us," observes Canadian artist and autism rights campaigner Ralph Smith, "I still believe that media will be the deciding factor in whether or not autistic people are granted human rights. Currently we're losing badly" (Ralph Smith, personal communication).

Smith's assertion that those with autism are 'losing' in the battle over how the condition is being represented is further evidence that the assertion that the condition can be cured is still a mainstream position. There is nothing unusual, it appears, in suggesting that a cure for autism is a good idea, a viewpoint returned to with regularity by the media. Possibly nowhere are the politics of the topic more impassioned than in the discussions surrounding prenatal testing, where the potential of research to develop *in utero* testing for genetic difference offers the opportunity to imagine a future in which fetal selection is a reality. There is a genuine feeling of unease surrounding all aspects of genetic screening; the acknowledgment of the possibilities provided by science is countered by the worry that the process might license dangerous selection practices. With autism, the situation is complicated by current ignorance of the full genetic pathways that might be responsible for the condition's development, and its characterization as a spectrum. If it were ever possible to determine that a fetus might display a genetic predisposition to autism, what kind of autism would it be? Given that there is considerable difference between 'classic' autism and Asperger's Syndrome, trying to identify specifics of the condition through prenatal screening may well be akin to attempting to shoot one out of hundreds of rapidly moving targets—blindfolded and in the dark.

But the debate goes on. In 2007, Nobel laureate James Watson, famed as one of the discoverers of the structure of DNA in 1953, commented in an interview that the possibility of screening for autism might prevent what he termed the "horror and destruction" that comes with the condition. "We might prevent," he went on, "some [autism-prone] families having subsequent children" (Hunt-Grubbe 2007, 31). Watson's comments on autism went largely unnoticed because, in the same interview, he also observed that people of African descent were

Figure 3.4 Ralph Smith, *Baby*: Smith's work challenges a majority view of autism through the use of unsettling images

© Ralph Smith

genetically inferior (he stated that "all our social policies are based on the fact that their intelligence is the same as ours—whereas all the testing says not really" [Hunt-Grubbe 2007, 33]). Watson was forced to resign as the chancellor of a major US research laboratory because of his comments on race, but although he has been represented as an iconoclast and a maverick, his position on autism and genetics, and his misinformation about the topic, is not unique.

In January 2009, major news outlets in the UK picked up on research conducted by Simon Baron-Cohen's team at Cambridge and revealed that high levels of testosterone in the amniotic fluid surrounding the

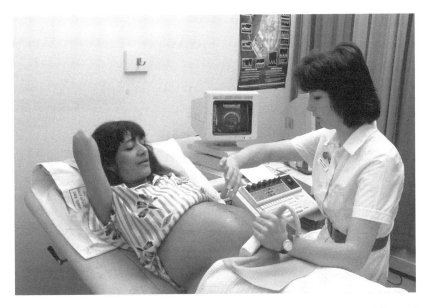

Figure 3.5 The possibility of prenatal testing for autism is one of the most controversial current debates surrounding the condition

© Anthea Sieveking/Wellcome Images

fetus in the womb might serve as some kind of early indication of autism. According to the headline in *The Independent* newspaper, this prompted "The Big Question: should mothers be offered screening for autism, and what issues would it raise?" (Laurence 2009). For its part, *The Guardian* newspaper asserted that "New research brings autism screening close to reality," with the feature article written by the paper's health editor noting that the research would inevitably provoke calls "for a national debate about the consequences of screening for the disorder in the womb and allowing women to terminate babies with the condition" (Boseley 2009). All the media outlets that ran the study highlighted the controversy of the issue, invoking both the 'tragedy' scenario of individual and family lives blighted by autism, and the risk of losing high-functioning or savant individuals (Einstein and Newton were cited) if termination was allowed: "A Prenatal Test for Autism would Deprive the World of Future Geniuses" was the title of *The Guardian*'s science blog on the day it ran the feature (Randerson 2009).

If there was a degree of feverish excitement about the possibility of a testosterone test allowing for *in utero* detection of autism, a significant problem emerged in the days following the news. Having read the pieces in a number of the papers, in which he was frequently quoted, Baron-Cohen immediately wrote a response in which he pointed out that *all* the major claims of the head- and tag-lines in the various articles, and much of the coverage on the inside pages, was incorrect. "The new research was not about autism screening," he observed, adding: "the new research has not discovered that a high level of testosterone in prenatal tests is an indicator of autism; autism spectrum disorder has not been linked to high levels of testosterone in the womb; and tests (of autism) do not allow termination of pregnancies." Indeed, as Baron-Cohen pointed out, the research in question "did not even test children with autism" at all. Following up on the article, Baron-Cohen wrote in the *New Scientist* about the "blatant distortions" in the newspapers, and observed that the desire for "a simple, bite-size but inaccurate message" had totally misrepresented the nature of the actual research that had been undertaken (Murray 2010).

This particular piece of media reporting is instructive. It shows that the excitement surrounding the possibility of genetic testing is palpable. It works not only in terms of drama, but also through an appeal to an idea of some form of public benefit, that the eradication of autism will be better for all concerned. "Autism is a condition that renders both children and parents helpless," wrote *TopNews* blogger Jonathan Sanders in a piece on genetic testing for the condition in March 2010. "While the child has no idea what to do, think, say or feel" he continued, "the parents are devastated and have no idea how they can help their child." Sanders' characterization of autism as a disaster is relentless: "Autism is a difficult and harsh condition, which upsets children, their parents, friends, family and just about everybody." But the "new hope" that new research offers, he adds, could change this. The condition, he announces, can be "made better . . . thanks to the amazing gene test!" (J. Sanders 2010). What Sanders and the UK news example have in common, despite coming from very different kinds of sources, is a comprehensive misunderstanding of what actually constitutes genetic research into autism. Work being undertaken by research associations such as the Autism Genome Project, a multinational collection of scientists investigating the genetic basis of autism, is often the source for the news reports we have just seen. It is necessarily painfully slow, identifying potential gene combinations that suggest avenues of further exploration. It is a kind of mapping, and correspondingly as faulting as any exercise in cartography. The way in which the message is delivered, however, is indicative of real confusion about the issues involved; the manner in which reports abandon the detail of the research for an assumption of the banner headline produces what is often an outright fiction. The gap between the 'facts' of science here, and the 'facts' as they are reported, is substantial.

It is the consequences of being on the receiving end of this kind of confusion that makes many families, increasingly gaining their information on autism through web browsing, push for a cure to the condition that seems to be just around the corner. At the same time, those who have the condition warn of what they believe to be a clear eugenic impulse in the increased discussion of genetic screening. A number of the autism associations that seek respect for neurodiversity refer to those who seek to cure the condition, whether ante- or post-natal, as 'curebies,' a word that has entered the pro-rights lexicon. Discussion boards are full of links made between curebie philosophy and the Nazis and other eugenic movements. Amanda Baggs, one of the most articulate advocates of autistic integrity, has collected a number of articles on curebie thinking in the Information Library section of the autistics.org website. Baggs writes:

> If you are working toward cure or prevention and believe that you are acting out of love or devotion, please realize that the love and devotion are dangerously misguided, and change what you are doing. It is extremely difficult to realize that what you have been doing is hurting other people, particularly when you think you are acting out of a strong love and value for the same people. But working toward cure and prevention is hurting a *lot* of people, and a lot is at stake. What may be thought to arise out of love and devotion, winds up bearing a striking resemblance to hate.
>
> (Baggs 2010)

The criticism leveled at figures such as Baggs is that they do not represent those with autism who are incapable of speaking for themselves due to the severity of their disability. Some, especially the parents of children with autism, see the pro-rights activists as being arrogant in their assumption of the position from which they comment. Countering this, advocates point out that they have coherent and developed arguments about all aspects of autism, and that cure policies are not in the best interests of any individual with the condition. They also contest the idea of what constitutes 'severity': Baggs herself is largely non-verbal and prefers to communicate through writing, a choice common to a number of people with autism, many of whom may well be viewed as being severely disabled if judged by their behavioral characteristics. The idea of 'defeating' autism is, for Baggs, the taking of "steps toward the genetic elimination of autistic people—people like me—from the planet" (Baggs 2010).

There is no sign that the arguments surrounding curing autism will diminish. Indeed, as genetic research proceeds we should probably expect them to increase, especially because the development of scientific thinking on autism is paralleled by the growth of commentary on such thought by those who have the condition. It is possibly an irony that this stand-off is itself taking place at a time when the idea of an autism spectrum is recognized as never before and that, for all the problems surrounding misrepresentation, the public at large is becoming more used to the verbal and articulate person with autism as an example of someone with the condition. Such increased awareness might suggest that opposition to the idea of termination produced by genetic screening will increase, but the arguments that there are different *types* of autism, and the ongoing revelation of the details of the condition's genetic profile, could well mitigate against this.

We noted at the start of this section that autism cannot be cured, but possibly the fact that we are still in the early history of our understanding of the condition will reveal this to be a point about vocabulary. Maybe those who believe in curing will come to say that they actually mean 'changing,' eliminating the worst features of autism to preserve the best, and that ameliorative treatment programs may come from this. Advocates for the condition, and others, will say that this is impossible, that such an idea is still fundamentally eugenic. At the same time, if we come to accept the integrity of a life with autism, then the aggressive ideas surrounding change might diminish. It is probable however that the argument will be complicated by the recognition of many autisms, and even the division of the category 'autistic' to more accurately reflect the kinds of humanity the term might encompass (the rumors that those assembling *DSM-V* are considering abandoning the category of Asperger's Syndrome and drawing up a more nuanced nomenclature for diagnosing the autism spectrum are exactly part of such a possible revision). Where those that champion curing are definitely in the wrong is in their idea that somehow the autistic and the human can be kept apart, and that to eradicate the former is to liberate the latter. This is one of the worst by-products of the notion that the condition is some kind of toxin or malign 'visitation.' It is nothing of the sort, and that is a fact that will have to be accepted. In the end, it is this position that those who wish for a cure will need to come to terms with.

What *kind* of human autism might suggest, however, is an altogether different question. To acknowledge that there is no division between autism and 'the human' is to raise serious and substantial issues about how, as a culture or society, we come to define ourselves. Even as we are immersed in the arguments of the present, arguments we know to be explicable and vital, might we not also gesture toward a future in which autism plays a part in thinking about our common humanity? For decades, it was assumed that autism was such a disabling condition that it, and those diagnosed with it, were of no use. What if, however, autism, along with those who are autistic, proves to be central to the ways in which we conceive of our fundamental sense of self? How controversial might that be?

17 Conclusion

Autism and the Human—Again

It would not be wrong to feel that controversy dominates the ways in which we discuss autism at the moment, whatever claims we might choose to make about scientific or social progress. However much those involved in the debates might wish such controversies would end, they have stubbornly refused to go away. It might seem difficult to look towards the ways in which understanding autism might develop from such a position of uncertainty, but it is not an impossibility. And the question of the relationship between autism and the human is exactly the kind of space where an imaginative conception of such possibility might exist.

In trying to explain or describe the experience of having autism, one of the most oft-repeated assertions is that it is like being an alien. Those with the condition often say that living in the majority world makes them feel alien. They struggle in decoding the subtle clues that others use naturally when stating logic, or pursuing social communication, for example. The idea can be traced back to a remark made to the neurologist Oliver Sacks by Temple Grandin, one the most famous autists and a prolific writer and commentator on many subjects connected to the condition. "Much of the time," Grandin told Sacks, "I feel like an anthropologist on Mars" (Sacks 1995, 248). Sacks was sufficiently taken by the phrase to use it as the title for his 1995 collection of case studies on individuals with a variety of neurodiverse conditions, and the concept behind it has filtered down to more general usage: 'Martian' or alien difference seems an apt shorthand, for all that it is a little glib, to describe the disjuncture those with autism feel in their interactions with the non-autistic world. Equally, autists will sometimes note that it is others who are like aliens, so different are they from that which comes naturally to those who have the condition; and, for that majority of the population of course, it is autistic behavior that is the alien phenomenon and seems beyond understanding. In all cases, however, the same logic applies: the two communities are planets apart.

To be alien is necessarily not to be human. But how can we make an argument for autism as part of the pattern of human difference if we disallow those with the condition entry into the category in the first place? Ian Hacking, who has explored philosophical issues arising from the notion that autism constitutes some form of alien subjectivity, wonders if in fact the yoking together of the two terms says less about autism "than what it reveals about what it is to be human" (Hacking 2009, 44). In other words, despite what might seem to be an unbridgeable distance between the human and the alien, each position has a number of points of contact with the other. Possibly here we have a more appropriate metaphor for autism than many of those that currently circulate: a condition that seems unconnected to the core experience of humanity but in fact, when we look closer, is an example of exactly that.

As we touched upon in Part I, there is another context, and another set of details, that also invoke a relationship between the alien and autism. This is the sphere of the posthuman, especially as it is articulated through ideas of the relationship between humans and machines, technologies, and information systems, an interaction that leads to multiple questions concerning embodiment and the connections between people and their environment. Many who work in Disability Studies are drawn to the category of the posthuman, since it offers a potential subject position that includes the disabled body and mind precisely because of its critique of humanism (arguably, it is the force of humanist thinking that creates the language that sees autism in terms of suffering or tragedy, explicit 'human' elements). A posthuman body might be a disabled body, and if—as some assert—we live in a posthuman world, then that world can be one where disability is central and not peripheral. As a specific case in point, autism seems especially suited to this line of thinking because of its own associations with technology, particularly systems of computing or processing, and with objects. The fascination with the cyborg that is typical of posthuman thinking maybe suggests a kind of autistic-being-in-the-world; if the alien and the human are not held apart but actually inform each other, then the hybrid that results could possibly be read in terms of autism. Equally, the fact that some with the condition prefer objects to people seems an uncanny echo of the embodied relationship with our environment that posthumanism explores. Posthuman thought also includes theories taken from evolutionary biology, especially a call to understand the long history of biological evolution. The ways in which being human only includes a fraction of such evolution, such thinking asserts, means the state must be assumed to change as the future develops. Again, this strand sits well with the idea of a future in which we display greater understanding of neurodiversity informed, in part, by what autism has taught us.

These are heady ideas, and will be controversial to some, but they are in no way outlandish or fictional. Rather there is a clear logic to them, from the admittance that metaphors of autism and the alien abound to the fact that we know our own lives are integrated into technological and information systems as never before. The question that might be asked in response to this thinking is: where does this leave the lives of those with autism? For some, this very enquiry might smack of a humanist concern with a certain idea of 'life,' but it is not illegitimate, given our current position in trying to understand autism, to want to focus on improving the situation of those who still find themselves misunderstood and subject to prejudice. The answer to the question does not simply pit the supposed integrity of the lived life against the perceived vagaries of theory however; it is more complicated than that. Circulated through education, the kind of posthuman philosophizing outlined above can have real effects on those with autism in the ways in which it potentially opens up an idea of an inclusive future. Correspondingly, a misguided concentration on the lives of those with the condition might reinforce and perpetuate the all-too-familiar ideas of pity or loss that lead to isolation and rejection. And, of course, we need to acknowledge that there are people with autism who have opinions about these matters as well: as mentioned previously, one of the subjects often 'outed' in the literature of retrospective diagnosis is Ludwig Wittgenstein and, although this is a genuine flight of fancy, it would surely be enlightening to know his thoughts on the subject.

We might express it in this way: because of its difference, autism has the potential to renegotiate the terms of the human. As a condition, it is human in every aspect of its manifestation; as an example of the *diversity* of humankind, it possesses the ability to offer a critique of those lazy assertions of, and appeals to, a 'shared humanity,' to replace that strand of humanist thought that in its totalizing ideologies created the disabled subject, and to counter it with a radical notion of human difference and potential. The link between this idea of difference and a reconfigured idea of the human is clear, as the potential identified here is also a space of negotiation between our present and our future, a process that faces forward precisely because it opens up the category of 'the human.' If this is what we might learn by thinking through what it means to consider those with autism as aliens, and by acknowledging the integrity of autistic lives, then we could—together—all go a very long way indeed.

AFTERWORD

AUTISTIC PRESENCE

Most of this book was written in the summer of 2010, often during the early morning when I would get up to work in the hope that I would be able to produce my daily word target before my son, on his school vacation, himself appeared from his room. Usually he was up early too, so often the thinking and writing took place with the two of us together and would be punctuated by occasional checks on his early morning routine, or in responding to his requests for food and drink or to change a DVD. I have always thought that the predominant issue raised by autism is the sheer fact of its *presence*; it is here and will always be so. Such presence is the final yardstick by which all the various attempts to understand or interpret it, whether made through science or metaphor, are to be measured. And although we are right to want to generalize about it, and to discuss it in broad terms, it is also essential to recognize that it is always in personal form, always individual. It cannot be avoided, but rather invites and demands attention and response.

Both the American photographer Timothy Archibald and the Australian poet Les Murray also have sons with autism. In his 2010 collection *Echolilia*, Archibald captures his son in a variety of images, all united by his interaction with the world around him. In *Home Made Sunset 2008*, Elijah Archibald lies on the floor, watching the refraction of torchlight through plastic water bottles. It is a complex construction, geometric and precise, but its effect appears to be one of comfort, with

Elijah content in his appreciation of the moment he has created. In its sense of quiet privacy, the image is also one of *normality*; this is clearly autistic difference, but it is also an everyday moment, a small event in the daily business of an autistic life.

For his part, Murray has a poem entitled 'It Allows a Portrait in Line Scan at Fourteen' in which it is the condition itself, conceived of as a presence and the 'It' of the title, that 'allows' Murray's son, Alexander, to express himself. At times, the autism is controlling: "It requires rulings," Murray writes, and "It does not allow proportion." "It still runs him around the house," he observes; but, while running around the house, Murray's son is "cooing and laughing," and though the autism is never unproblematic for him—"*Don't say word!* When he was eight he forbade the word 'autistic' in his presence"—it also allows him knowledge and insight: "He remembers all the breeds of fowls," Murray writes, "and all the counties of Ireland"; "He has forgotten nothing, and remembers the precise quality of experiences." In a nice touch Murray notes that Alexander "climbed all over the dim Freudian psychiatrist who told us how autism resulted from 'refrigerator' parents" (Murray 1996, 49–50).

Figure 4.1 *Home Made Sunset 2008*
© Timothy Archibald

Murray's own precision in capturing the experience of autism is the product of a substantial creative imagination. In his poem, the condition is not one entity, nor does it take straightforward manifestations. It is complex, sometimes worrying and sometimes enlightening. But, as with Archibald's image, the poem is written from a viewpoint that is prepared to listen to autism, to gauge what it allows, and then to live with that. Both photograph and poem acknowledge the presence of the condition, and don't seek to make it something it is not. For a long time many people with autism were institutionalized, locked away from a public that could not even begin to understand them because it never saw them. That is no longer the case; there are now more autistic people than ever to meet, to spend time with, to help, to learn from, and to listen to. All these activities are part of everyday life, the normal activities of our world. Possibly understanding autism and getting beyond the facts through which it is too often reduced is, finally, simply about realizing that this is the case.

BIBLIOGRAPHY

Asperger, Hans. 1991. "'Autistic psychopathy' in childhood." In *Autism and Asperger Syndrome*, edited by Uta Frith, 37–92. Cambridge, UK: Cambridge University Press.

Aspies For Freedom. 2010. "Welcome to AFF." Accessed August 4, 2010. http://www.aspiesforfreedom.com.

Autism Speaks. 2010. "What We Fund and How We Fund It." Accessed July 27, 2010. http://www.autismspeaks.org/science/research/grants/index.php.

Autistic Self Advocacy Network (ASAN). 2010. "Public Policy." Accessed August 4, 2010. http://www.autisticadvocacy.org/modules/smartsection/category.php?categoryid=11.

Baggs, Amanda. 2007. "In My Language." Accessed September 16, 2010. http://www.youtube.com/watch?v=JnylMlh12jc.

Baggs, Amanda. 2010. "Love, Devotion, Hope, Prevention and Cure." Accessed August 23, 2010. http://www.autistics.org/library/love.html.

Barnbaum, Deborah R. 2008. *The Ethics of Autism: Among Them, but not of Them.* Bloomington & Indianapolis: Indiana University Press.

Baron-Cohen, Simon. 1995. *Mindblindness: An Essay on Autism and Theory of Mind.* Cambridge, MA: Bradford MIT Press.

Baron-Cohen, Simon. 2003. *The Essential Difference: Men, Women and the Extreme Male Brain.* London: Penguin/Allen Lane.

Baron-Cohen, Simon. 2008. *Autism and Asperger Syndrome.* Oxford, UK: Oxford University Press.

Bettelheim, Bruno. 1967. *The Empty Fortress: Infantile Autism and the Birth of the Self.* New York: Free Press/Macmillan.

Biklen, Douglas. 2005. *Autism and the Myth of the Person Alone.* New York and London: New York University Press.

Bogdan, Robert. 1990. *Freak Shows: Presenting Human Oddities for Amusement and Profit.* Chicago and London: University of Chicago Press.

Boseley, Sarah. 2009. "New Research Brings Autism Screening Closer to Reality." *The Guardian*, January 12. Accessed January 13, 2009. http://www.guardian.co.uk/lifeandstyle/2009/jan/12/autism-screening-health.

Bouthiena, Jemel, Laurent Mottron, and Michelle Dawson. 2006. "Impaired Face Processing in Autism: Fact or Artifact?" *Journal of Autism and Developmental Disorders* 36 (1): 91–106.

Brown, Julie. 2010. *Writers on the Spectrum: How Autism and Asperger Syndrome have Influenced Literary Writing.* London and Philadelphia: Jessica Kingsley.

Collins, Paul. 2004. *Not Even Wrong: A Father's Journey into the Lost History of Autism.* New York and London: Bloomsbury.

Conrad, Joseph. 1898. *Tales of Unrest.* London: Eveleigh, Nash & Grayson.

Dapretto, M., M. Davies, J.H. Pfeifer, A.A. Scott, M. Sigman, S.Y. Bookheimer, and M. Iacoboni, 2006. "Understanding Emotions in Others: fMRI Evidence of Mirror Neuron Dysfunction in Children with Autism Spectrum Disorders." *Nature Neuroscience* 9: 28–30.

Dawson, Michelle, Isabelle Soulières, Morton Ann Gernsbacher, and Laurent Mottron. 2007. "The Level and Nature of Autistic Intelligence." *Psychological Science* 18 (8): 657–62.

Donovan, John and Caren Zucker. 2010. "Autism's First Child." *The Atlantic.* October. Accessed September 10, 2010. http://www.theatlantic.com/magazine/archive/2010/10/autism-8217-s-first-child/8227/3/.

DSM-IV-TR: Diagnostic and Statistical Manual of Mental Disorders. 2000. Fourth Edition. Text Revision. Arlington, VA: American Psychiatric Association.

Ecker, Christine, Andre Marquand et al. 2010. "Describing the Brain in Autism in Five Dimensions—Magnetic Resonance Imaging-Assisted of Autism Spectrum Disorders Using a Multiparameter Classification Approach." *Journal of Neuroscience* 30 (32): 10612–23.

Feinstein, Adam. 2010. *A History of Autism: Conversations with the Pioneers.* Chichester, UK: Wiley-Blackwell.

Fitzgerald, Michael. 2004. *Autism and Creativity: Is There a Link between Autism and Men and Exceptional Ability?* London and Philadelphia: Jessica Kingsley.

Fitzgerald, Michael. 2005. *The Genesis of Artistic Creativity: Asperger's Syndrome and the Arts.* London and Philadelphia: Jessica Kingsley.

Frith, Uta. 1989. *Autism: Explaining the Enigma.* Oxford, UK: Basil Blackwell.

Frith, Uta. 2008. *Autism: A Very Short Introduction.* Oxford, UK: Oxford University Press.

Gajilan, A. Chris. 2007. "Living with Autism in a World Made for Others." Accessed September 16, 2010. http://www.cnn.com/2007/HEALTH/02/21/autism.amanda/index.html.

Garland-Thomson, Rosemarie. 1997. *Extraordinary Bodies: Figuring Physical Disability in American Culture and Literature.* New York: Columbia University Press.

Generation Rescue. 2010. "Jenny McCarthy's Autism Organization—Generation Rescue." Accessed August 10, 2010. http://www.generationrescue.org.

Gernsbacher, Morton Ann, Michelle Dawson, and H. Hill Goldsmith. 2005. "Three Reasons not to Believe in an Autism Epidemic." *Current Directions in Psychological Science* 14 (2): 55–58.

Grandin, Temple. 2005. *Animals in Translation: Using the Mysteries of Autism to Decode Animal Behavior.* London: Bloomsbury.

Grandin, Temple. 2006. Second Edition. *Thinking in Pictures, and Other Reports from My Life with Autism.* London: Bloomsbury.

Grandin, Temple and Margaret M. Scariano. 2005. Second Edition. *Emergence: Labeled Autistic—A True Story.* New York: Warner Books.

Grinker, Roy Richard. 2007. *Unstrange Minds: Remapping the World of Autism*. New York: Basic Books.

Grinker, Roy Richard. 2010. "Commentary: On being Autistic, and Social." *Ethos* 38 (1): 172–78.

Gupta, Sanjay. 2007. "Behind the Veil of Autism." Accessed September 16, 2010. http://www.cnn.com/HEALTH/blogs/paging.dr.gupta/2007/02/behind-veil-of-autism.html.

Hacking, Ian. 2009. "Humans, Aliens & Autism." *Daedalus* Summer: 44–59.

Hacking, Ian. 2010. "Autism Fiction: The Mirror of an Internet Decade?" *University of Toronto Quarterly* 79 (2): 632–55.

Haddon, Mark. 2003. *The Curious Incident of the Dog in the Night-Time*. London: Jonathan Cape.

Halliwell, Martin. 2004. *Images of Idiocy: The Idiot Figure in Modern Fiction and Film*. Aldershot, UK: Ashgate.

Hunt-Grubbe, Charlotte. 2007. "The Elementary DNA of Dr. Watson." *The Sunday Times Magazine*, October 14: 24–33.

ICD-10: International Statistical Classification of Diseases and Related Health Problems. 2009. Tenth Revision. Volume 1. Geneva: World Health Organization.

Isaacson, Rupert. 2009. *The Horse Boy: The True Story of a Father's Miraculous Journey to Heal His Son*. London: Penguin.

Kanner, Leo. 1943. "Autistic Disturbances of Affective Contact." *Nervous Child* 2: 217–50.

Kaufman, Raun. 1994. "Foreword," in Barry Neil Kaufman, *Son-Rise: The Miracle Continues*. Tiburon, CA: H.J. Kramer/New World Library.

Kaufman, Sharon R. 2010. "Regarding the Rise in Autism: Vaccine Safety Doubt, Conditions of Inquiry, and the Shape of Freedom." *Ethos* 38 (1): 8–32.

Kirby, David. 2005. *Evidence of Harm—Mercury in Vaccines and the Autism Epidemic: A Medical Controversy*. New York: St. Martin's Press.

Laurence, Jeremy. 2009. "The Big Question: Should Mothers be Offered Screening for Autism, and What Issues would It Raise?" *The Independent*. January 13. Accessed January 14, 2009. http://www.independent.co.uk/extras/big-question/the-big-question-should-mothers-be-offered-screening-for-autism-and-what-issues-would-it-raise-1332040.html.

Liu, Ka-Yuet, Marissa King, and Peter S. Bearman. 2010. "Social Influence and the Autism Epidemic." *American Journal of Sociology* 115 (5): 1387–434.

Lovaas, O. Ivar. 1987. "Behavioral Treatment and Normal Educational and Intellectual Functioning in Young Autistic Children." *Journal of Consulting and Clinical Psychology* 55 (1): 3–9.

Mottron, Laurent, Michelle Dawson, Isabelle Soulières, Benedicte Hubert, and Jane Burack. 2006. "Enhanced Perceptual Functioning in Autism: An Update, and Eight Principles of Autistic Perception." *Journal of Autism and Developmental Disorders* 36 (1): 27–43.

Mukhopadhyay, Tito Rajarshi. 2003. *The Mind Tree: A Miraculous Child Breaks the Silence of Autism*. New York: Arcade.

Mukhopadhyay, Tito Rajarshi. 2008. *How Can I Talk if My Lips don't Move? Inside My Autistic Mind*. New York: Arcade.

Mukhopadhyay, Tito Rajarshi and Soma Mukhopadhyay. 2005. *The Gold of the Sunbeams, and Other Stories*. New York: Arcade.

Murray, Les. 1996. "It Allows a Portrait in Line-Scan at Fourteen." *Subhuman Redneck Poems*. Potts Point, NSW: Duffy & Snellgrove.

Murray, Stuart. 2008. *Representing Autism*. Liverpool, UK: Liverpool University Press.

Murray, Stuart. 2010. "Autism Functions/The Function of Autism." *Disability Studies Quarterly* 30 (1). Accessed March 15, 2010. http://www.dsq-sds.org/article/view/1048/1229.

Nadesan, Majia Holmer. 2005. *Constructing Autism: Unravelling the "Truth" and Understanding the Social*. New York: Routledge.

Nazeer, Kamran. 2006. *Send in the Idiots: Stories from the Other Side of Autism*. London: Bloomsbury.

Norden, Martin F. 1994. *The Cinema of Isolation: A History of Physical Disability in the Movies*. New Brunswick, NJ: Rutgers University Press.

Offit, Paul. 2008. *Autism's False Prophets: Bad Science, Risky Medicine and the Search for a Cure*. New York: Columbia University Press.

Osteen, Mark, ed. 2008. *Autism and Representation*. New York: Routledge.

Osteen, Mark. 2010. *One of Us: A Family's Life with Autism*. Columbia and London: University of Missouri Press.

Randerson, James. 2009. "A Prenatal Test for Autism would Deprive the World of Future Geniuses." *The Guardian Science Blog*. January 12. Accessed January 12, 2010. http://www.guardian.co.uk/science/blog/2009/jan/07/autism-test-genius-dirac.

Rose, Brian. 2010. "Brain Scan to detect Autism will Ease Diagnosis and Save NHS Money." *The Times*, August 11.

Russell, James, ed. 1997. *Autism as an Executive Disorder*. Oxford, UK: Oxford University Press.

Sacks, Oliver. 1995. *An Anthropologist on Mars*. London: Picador.

Sanders, Jonathan. 2010. "Genetic Testing for Autism: We Were Waiting!" *Jonathan Sanders's TopNews blog*. March 17. Accessed August 10, 2010. http://topnews.us/content/213407-genetic-testing-autism-we-were-waiting.

Sanders, Lisa. 2010. *Diagnosis: Dispatches from the Frontlines of Medical Mysteries*. London: Icon Books.

Savarese, Ralph James. 2007. *Reasonable People: A Memoir of Autism & Adoption*. New York: Other Press.

Schreibman, Laura. 2005. *The Science and Fiction of Autism*. Cambridge, MA and London: Harvard University Press.

Simmons, James Q. and O. Ivar Lovaas. 1969. "Use of Pain and Punishment as Treatment Techniques with Childhood Schizophrenics." *American Journal of Psychotherapy* 23 (1): 23–36.

Sinclair, Jim. 1993. *Our Voice*, 1 (3): n.p.

Smith, Ralph, personal communication to author, Feb. 9, 2008.

Sontag, Susan. 1991. *Illness as Metaphor & Aids and its Metaphors*. London: Penguin.

Wakefield, A.J, S.H. Murch et al. 1998. "Illeal-lymphoid-nodular hyperplasia, non-specific colitis, and pervasive developmental disorder in children." *Lancet* 351 (9103): 637–41.

Waldman, Michael, Sean Nicholson, Nodir Adilov, and John Williams. 2008. "Autism Prevalence and Precipitation Rates in California, Oregon, and Washington Counties." *Archives of Pediatrics and Adolescent Medicine* 162 (11): 1026–34.

Wallis, Claudia. 2006. "Does Watching TV Cause Autism?" *Time*, October 20. Accessed July 14, 2010. http://www.time.com/time/health/article/0,8599,1548682,00.html.

Weber, Wendy and Sanford Newmark. 2007. "Complementary and Alternative Medical Therapies for Attention-Deficit/Hyperactivity Disorder and Autism." *Pediatric Clinics of North America* 54 (6): 983–1006.

Williams, Donna. 1992. *Nobody Nowhere: The Extraordinary Autobiography of an Autistic*. New York: Times Books.

Williams, Donna. 1994. *Somebody Somewhere: Breaking Free from the World of Autism*. New York: Times Books.

Wing, Lorna and Judith Gould. 1979. "Severe Impairments of Social Interaction and Associated Abnormalities in Children: Epidemiology and Classification." *Journal of Child Psychology and Psychiatry* 18: 167–78.

INDEX

Page numbers in *italics* denote an illustration